ROMAN
CHICHESTER

Aerial view of Chichester.

ROMAN CHICHESTER

Alec Down

Phillimore

1988
Published by
PHILLIMORE & CO. LTD.
Shopwyke Hall, Chichester, Sussex

ISBN 0 85033 435 7

Phototypeset by Input Typesetting Ltd, London.
Printed and bound in Great Britain by
UNWIN BROTHERS LTD.
Old Woking, Surrey

Contents

List of Illustrations

Frontispiece: Aerial view of Chichester

Illustration Acknowledgements

John Adams, nos. 19, 34, 36 and 74; Chichester District Museum, nos. 18, 26 and 53; G. Claridge, nos. 8, 14, 16, 45, 50, 51, 70, 73 and 79; J. Hinde, no. 28; Adrian Lack, no. 27; J. J. O'Hea, frontispiece and no. 39; Raymond Thomas, nos. 29, 30a, 30b and 81; T. Westmore, nos. 2 and 60; Robert Wilkins (Institute of Archaeology, Oxford), no. 61. All other photographs are the author's own.

Acknowledgements

The author acknowledges with thanks the assistance given by the following people in the preparation of this volume for press and also those people and organisations who have kindly given permission for illustrations to be used: The Curator and Staff of Chichester District Museum, Christopher Down, Yvonne Gooding, John Piper (drawing), Raymond Thomas, Thelma and Graham Westmore (photography), Max Wholey (reconstructions); Professor B. W. Cunliffe and the Society of Antiquaries of London (Fishbourne Vol. 1), The Council for British Archaeology (Research Report No. 29), The Chichester District Archaeological Advisory Committee (*Chichester Excavations* 1–6), A. King & G. Soffe (The Hayling Island Temple), F. G. Aldsworth (Bignor and West Marden Roman Villa plans), D. J. Rudkin (The Roman building at Fishbourne creek).

Museums with Collections of Roman Material
from Chichester and District

Chichester District Museum: Little London, Chichester. Open Tuesday to Saturday from 10 a.m.

Bignor Roman Villa: Bignor, West Sussex. Open March to October (Tuesday-Sunday) from 10 a.m.

Fishbourne Roman Palace: Fishbourne, Chichester. Houses the finest collection of first-century mosaics in Britain and now exhibits the mosaics from Chilgrove 1 and St Peter's, Chichester. Open from 1 March to 30 November every day. December, January and February – Sundays only.

List of Abbreviations

R.R.S.A.L.	Research Report of the Society of Antiquaries of London
S.A.C.	Sussex Archaeological Collections
S.N.Q.	Sussex Notes and Queries (previously published by the Sussex Archaeological Society)
Proc. Soc. Antiq.	Proceedings of the Society of Antiquaries
V.C.H.	Victoria County History (Sussex)
Ant. J.	Antiquaries Journal
P.P.S.	Proceedings of the Prehistoric Society
B.A.R.	British Archaeological Reports

Author's Note

This is the second work on Roman Chichester to be published within the last 23 years. The first, 'Chichester: the Roman Town', published by John Holmes M.A., F.S.A. as *Chichester Paper* No. 50, summarised what was known of the town through his own, and earlier, excavations and chance discoveries. This volume takes the process several stages further and embraces, as far as possible, all the work in and around the *civitas* capital which has been carried out up to 1987, and includes a number of sites which have not yet been published.

The book has been five years in the making, mainly because of the immense pressures of urgent rescue excavation at the Cattlemarket, Fishbourne (A27), Theological College and Appledown sites and the need constantly to revise my conclusions in the light of new discoveries. My first thanks are therefore due to my publishers for their forbearance.

It is not primarily for archaeologists, although I hope that many will find it useful; but for the interested layman who wishes to learn more about the past without wading through the minutiae of archaeological excavation reports, which are mainly intended to enlighten (or confuse) other archaeologists. It does not purport to be the final word on the subject. Chichester is still under attack by developers and the motor car, and new discoveries will inevitably be made which will cause some of the present conclusions to be modified or discarded.

I owe much to discussions with colleagues and I am particularly grateful to John Magilton, my successor as Director of the Chichester Archaeological Unit, and to Dr. Martin Henig and Julian Munby who read parts or all of the draft manuscript and made a number of helpful comments. I must, however, reserve to myself the responsibility for any errors which remain.

Chapter One

Roman Chichester

The background to the Invasion; Atrebates and Catuvellauni

The story of Roman Chichester begins in the late Iron Age and in order to understand its origins we should first look at what happened in the period immediately prior to the Roman invasion of A.D. 43. The political and military ambitions of the shadowy personalities who ruled the tribes in Britain in the late 1st century B.C. and the military response by Rome to the destabilising effect of Catuvellaunian aggression in the south-east all had an influence on the decision to build a town on the site where Chichester now is.

By the end of the 1st century B.C. the names of the Iron Age tribes in south-east Britain are known and the territory that they occupied can be conjectured. It must be said at the outset that much of the evidence for this depends heavily on the distribution of coins minted by the various tribal rulers, some of whom are mentioned in contemporary Roman literature. In addition, some of the towns and strongpoints occupied by the tribes have been identified, particularly those which later became Roman regional capitals. Some of the Belgic tribes, who emigrated to Britain from Gaul in the earlier part of the 1st century B.C. and superimposed themselves on the local tribes in the south and east, had territory on both sides of the Channel, and it was to Britain that many of the dissident elements in Gaul fled after Caesar's conquest there. In Gaul, the Belgic leader Commius, who at first supported Caesar, later joined the revolt against him led by Vercingetorix. When this failed, he fled to Britain, probably about the middle of the 1st century B.C. Once here, he seems to have established a dynasty in the south-east and the tribe that he ruled is known to us as the Atrebates. They may originally have come from the Arras region of Gaul and in Britain they probably occupied the area of Sussex, Surrey and eastern Hampshire (Pl. 1). To the east, in Kent, were the Cantiaci, to the west, in Dorset, the Durotriges, with the Catuvellauni to the north and Trinovantes to the east in the area of the Home Counties north of the Thames. Nothing is known of the subsequent career of Commius after he had established his rule in southern Britain, but it cannot be doubted he was an important figure. He appears to have had three sons, Tincommius, who succeeded him as ruler; Eppillus, who is thought to have ruled for a time in Kent, and Verica, who may have succeeded or ousted Tincommius and who seems to have ruled the Atrebates for a considerable time, up to a few years before the invasion of A.D. 43, when he was forced to flee to Rome to ask for help against his northern neighbours, the Catuvellauni.

The sons of Commius took pride in claiming kinship with him, as can be seen from the coins they struck, which often carry the legend 'Commi F or CF' (Commi Filius), (Pl. 2). Two of the coins of Verica found in Chichester in recent years are of particular interest. Both are tiny silver minims of hitherto unknown types and were found below the Central Girls School in Chapel Street[1] in levels associated with the early military occupation. One (Pl. 2.5) has an ox-head on the reverse with the legend VERICA around it. The obverse carries the picture of a classical building with closed doors and

1

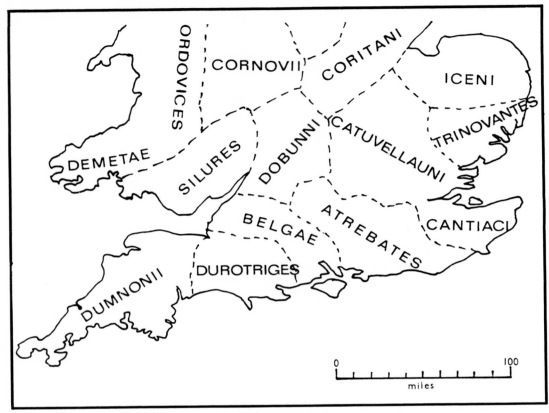

1. Iron Age tribal territories in southern Britain before the Roman Conquest.

the legend C – F, (Commi Filius). This might possibly be a representation of the tomb of Commius and perhaps the coin was struck as one of a series of memorial issues. The other coin is even more intriguing (Pl. 2.4). The reverse carries a winged horse (Pegasus) with the letters CO (for Commius), while the obverse has the letters VIR/ VAR. It is likely that the VIR stands for Verica and if this is correct then it is at least possible that VAR is a reference to Verica's oppidum or stronghold, which is presumed to have been at Selsey. This is incapable of proof, but some Catuvellaunian coins, struck by Cunobelin when his capital was at Camulodunum (Colchester), carry the legend CAM (Pl. 2.1) and Eppillus, who ruled the northern part of the Atrebatic territory, struck coins inscribed CALLEV (for Calleva) in the early part of the 1st century A.D., so it can be seen that the custom of identifying the ruler with his principle town on the coinage was well established in late Iron Age Britain.

Verica's northern capital may have originally been at Silchester (Calleva Atrebatum) and the town at Selsey may have served as the main port into the territory. There is no clear evidence for the existence of this town, but a considerable number of gold coins has been found on the beaches at Selsey, Bracklesham and Aldwick, as well as

2.   Early British coins from Chichester, all approx. 2/1.
(1) Bronze coin of Cunobelin (A.D. 10–40). *Reverse*: lion crouching, below tree; on a tablet below; CAM (for Camulodunum).
(2) Gold quarter stater of Eppillus. *Reverse*: CALL (for Calleva).
(3) Silver minim, probably of Amminius. *Obverse*: letter A in centre of two interlaced squares with curved sides. (4) Silver minim of Verica (new type). *Obverse*: VIR/VAR in two lines on tablet. *Reverse*: Pegasus to r; below, C O. (5) Silver minim of Verica (new type). *Obverse*: Bucranium, around VERICA. *Reverse*: Tomb or monumental altar; to l C: to r F.

some waste gold. These discoveries might point to the existence of a mint nearby, which would have functioned in or near to one of the main tribal administrative centres. A large amount of land has been lost to the sea at Selsey since Roman times and it is now difficult to envisage an Iron Age town with harbour facilities, but the nature of the finds and a study of the topography, especially when it is compared with the Iron Age site at Hengistbury Head in Dorset, make it a possibility which should not be dismissed out of hand.

North of Chichester (Pl. 3) are a series of linear defensive ditches known as the Chichester Dykes. They were not all constructed at once and there is some evidence that at the eastern end they were re-used in medieval times as park boundaries. They now appear to be discontinuous, but some of the gaps might have been filled by natural obstacles such as densely wooded areas, or certain lengths might never have been completed. Much has been written about the Dykes[2] which are similar to those at Lexden, near Colchester, and they are probably best seen as part of an Atrebatic defensive system, perhaps engineered by Verica at a time when he was being hard put

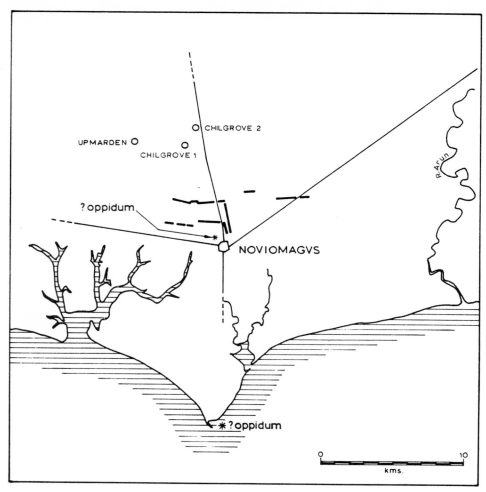

3. Map of south-west Sussex showing the relationship of Noviomagus to the dykes.

4. Part of an Iron Age roundhouse excavated at the Cattlemarket.

to it to maintain a foothold in Sussex. The ditches themselves were unlikely to have functioned, as Curwen suggested,[3] as anti-chariot defences and they are too extensive to have been continuously manned. It perhaps makes more sense to consider them as delimiting a part of the tribal territory, and the size and depth of the ditches when they were first dug would make it difficult for raiders to drive cattle out 'on the hoof'. As much of the wealth of Iron Age communities was in their cattle there would be a sound economic reason for constructing such massive earthworks.

It is likely that there were a number of villages or settlements within the boundaries of the Dykes and one of these may have been near to the Eastgate of the later Roman city, where plans of three circular huts have recently been found (Pl. 4). Trade with Rome in the half century or so before the invasion of A.D. 43 was quite brisk, with goods coming over from the Seine estuary to Chichester harbour or to the Selsey oppidum. Some of the pottery found below the Central Girls School in Chapel Street dated to the reign of Augustus, with one amphora which had contained wine being dated by the stamp on the handle to the late 1st century B.C. At the Eastgate Cattlemarket site, other amphorae dating to the same period have been identified – clear proof of trade with Gaul well before the invasion.

During the latter part of the reign of Augustus, the political situation in the south-east of Britain was becoming unstable from the Roman point of view. The Catuvellauni to the north of the Atrebatic territory appear to have expanded eastwards and taken over the territory of the Trinovantes (in Essex), and their king, Cunobelin, ruled from both Verulamium (by St. Albans) and Camulodunum (Colchester). Cunobelin (who can be equated with Shakespeare's Cymbeline) was the most powerful and important ruler in Britain and he was probably regarded as an ally of Rome although his expansionist policies seemed to be flouting the conditions of the treaty imposed on the tribe by Julius Caesar in 53 B.C.[4] Whilst he was alive there does not seem to have been any serious move against his southern neighbours, but after his death, when he was succeeded by his two sons Togodumnus and Caratacus, the situation worsened rapidly. Pressure was exerted on the Atrebates, and it seems that the northern capital Calleva (Silchester) fell to the Catuvellauni. Within a few years it appears likely that Verica's territory had shrunk to a small area along the Sussex coast, and eventually he gave up the unequal struggle and fled to Rome. Dio Cassius records the appearance of a 'Berikos' as a suppliant at the court of Claudius[5] and thereafter no more is heard of him. According to the coin evidence he probably ruled for about 40 years and must have been an old man when he went into exile. Although Commius had fled from the Romans after the unsuccessful uprising in Gaul in the previous century, the heirs to the kingdom he established on this side of the Channel seem to have developed pro-Roman sympathies with the passage of time and, with a strong Atrebatic ruler in the south-east of Britain, Rome could feel that the western flank was secure. The situation changed with the death of Cunobelin. His expansionist policy vis-a-vis the Trinovantes had been tolerated, but when his sons began to exert pressure on the Atrebates to the south, an action which culminated in the flight of Verica, it became clear that some decisive action was needed to stabilise a potentially dangerous situation. An invasion had been planned in A.D.40 when Caligula was Emperor but this had been abandoned when the legions mutinied. Claudius, who had succeeded as Emperor in A.D. 41 when his nephew was murdered, was anxious to prove himself and had a sound diplomatic reason for intervening in the affairs of Britain by helping an ally and restoring the balance of power in the south-east of the island. The invasion was set in train in A.D.43 and four legions set sail in three divisions, to land somewhere near Richborough in Kent. The possibility has been canvassed that one division was landed in Sussex, at Chichester harbour but, while a small detachment might have brought back the aged Verica to organise support among his fellow tribesmen and to influence tribes further to the west, it is unlikely that Aulus Plautius, the commander of the expedition, would have risked dividing his forces to any great extent at the beginning of a major campaign. Undoubtedly, the Romans knew a great deal about southern Britain from Caesar's campaigns and information gathered by traders, and the problems of penetrating northwards with a large force through the dense Wealden forest would have been appreciated.

It is known that a decisive battle was fought in Kent on the banks of a river which must have been the Medway. The Catuvellauni and their allies, led by the sons of Cunobelin, provided the main resistance to the invaders and after a two-day battle the British were defeated and retreated westwards, crossing the Thames. Togodumnus had been killed in skirmishing at this point, and after waiting for the Emperor Claudius to join the army from Gaul, Aulus Plautius advanced into Essex and took Camulodunum. This virtually marked the end of the campaign in the south-east and shortly afterwards the Second Legion (Legio II Augusta) under the command of the future Emperor Vespasian was detached southwards to prepare for the campaign to take the Isle of Wight and subdue the west country. This legion is known to have fought a number of battles and taken 20 native *oppida* or strongpoints and subdued two hostile tribes, one of which would have been the Durotriges in Dorset.[6]

The logical choice for the legion to set up its first base camp after reaching the south coast would have been in an area which offered good harbour facilities and a well-drained site within friendly territory. Where better than the coastal plain near Chichester harbour, where the Romans would be welcome as allies? Excavations at Fishbourne and Chichester leave little room for doubt that this was the site of the first base camp, with the port facilities and store-buildings at Fishbourne (and probably Dell Quay) and the legionary and auxiliary camps slightly to the east, where Chichester now is.

The military base

The main strategy for the conquest of the south-east had probably been settled in outline before the legions left Gaul and, once the Catuvellauni had been dealt with, the next move would be to prepare for the campaign to take the Isle of Wight as a prelude to the conquest of the west country. The choice of the Chichester area as the spring-board for mounting the attack must have been made very early on in the campaign and two of the chief reasons for selecting it would have been that it had a good harbour through which supplies could be brought from Gaul, and was in friendly territory (Pl. 3). It is likely, then, that an advance party was detached from Essex (probably by sea) as soon as the fighting was over, in order to get on with the job of planning the port facilities, marking out roads and choosing the actual sites for the troops to put up their tents. The legion probably marched down from Camulodunum and arrived in the late summer. Whether they went into action straightaway to take the Isle of Wight or whether they spent the rest of the campaigning season in setting up the camp and preparing their winter quarters is not known, but it would have been sound tactics, in view of the short sea crossing, for Vespasian to deal with the threat to his southern flank at the earliest possible time.

Legio II Augusta had already distinguished itself in the earlier fighting at the battle of the Medway. Its 34-year-old commander, T. Flavius Vespasianus, had risen from humble origins (his father was a tax gatherer) and had proved himself to be a competent and popular leader. His campaign westwards from Sussex was a 'copy book' operation in which first the Isle of Wight was taken and then, his southern flank secure, he advanced into the hostile territories of the Belgae and Durotriges. Eventually, the legion reached Exeter, but the time taken for this advance is not known. It might well have taken up two seasons of fighting and Vespasian's resources would have been well stretched by the need to set up garrisons at strategic points in the territory that had been overrun.

The full fighting strength of the legion would have been about 5,300 men, to which would be added auxiliary troops, both infantry and cavalry. These were normally organised in *cohorts* of 500 or 1,000 men if infantry, or *alae* of similar sizes if cavalry. Altogether, Vespasian probably had 8–10,000 men at his disposal including the administrative grades, whose job it was to see that the army got the supplies in the right place at the right time. Supplies and reinforcements would initially have come by sea from Gaul to Chichester harbour, and this arrangement may well have continued for some time after the advance westwards had lengthened the lines of communication between the base and the forward troops. Sea-borne supplies had to come in by the shortest practical route from the Seine estuary and then went westwards along the coast. Eventually, the main base at Chichester would have been too far from the scene of operations and its importance as a staging post would be diminished. It is possible that some form of depot might have remained for some time after A.D. 44 but the legion headquarters had probably gone within two years. There is no archaeological evidence in Chichester for a military presence lasting any length of time, and it would be very difficult to prove. However, it would have been strategically sound to leave a small garrison behind. The speed of Vespasian's advance must have meant that there were areas in the south and west that were not completely pacified and, while it is true that the southern Atrebates in the Chichester area were pro-Roman, the ruler on the spot, whether the aged Verica or the young Cogidubnus, might have needed some outside military support to cope with dissident elements. At the worst, British and Gaulish tribes being notoriously fickle in their alliegances, a military presence would provide some incentive to remain friendly to Rome.

We hear no more of Vespasian in Britain after this campaign, but his later career set the seal on his military reputation. He successfully put down the Jewish revolt during Nero's reign and finally, in A.D. 69 towards the end of the civil war, was proclaimed Emperor by the Army. He reigned for ten years and proved a just and popular ruler.

The evidence for the base camp

The Chichester area was a good choice for a base. The terrain was level, well drained and near to the harbour where supplies and reinforcements could be landed. In those days, two streams ran across the plain to the sea. The most easterly of the two, the River Lavant, may have flowed south-east into Pagham harbour, or taken a more circuitous route into Chichester harbour than it does now. It was re-routed to flow around the walls of Chichester at a later date. The western stream flowed south and west and emptied into the harbour. The area between the two streams was selected as the site for the legion and auxiliary troops and it can be seen from the plan (Pl. 5) that both 'legs' of the defensive ditch and all the finds of military equipment are within the area encompassed by the stream, which would have provided a source of water for the troops and also enhanced the defensive perimeter.

The full extent of the base at Chichester and Fishbourne may never be known, as most of it lies below streets and houses in the centre of the town and below areas covered by the Fishbourne palace. It was only in the years 1969–1977 that a sufficiently large area in the north-west quadrant of the town became available for development, and excavation in advance of building gave us the opportunity, for the first time, to have a really good view of what lay below the properties fronting on to Chapel Street, Crane Street and Tower Street. It was then that the ephemeral traces of the timber-framed barrack-like structures became apparent (Pl. 6, 7 & 8). The buildings showed only as stains in the clay sub-soil, but the regularity of the plan and the associated finds of military equipment leave little room for doubt that they had a military function. They are also similar in plan to barrack blocks found at legionary camps elsewhere. What is not clear is whether these buildings belonged to the base camp of A.D. 43–44 ot whether they were part of a depot remaining after the legion had departed.

Only the slots of the structures remained for the archaeologists to uncover. These were dug into the natural clay (Pl. 8) and the impressions of the posts which were placed upright in the slots could still be seen. Sometimes the slot housed a cill-beam which was pierced at intervals along its length to take the timber uprights. The stains in the clay left by the rotted beams can be detected by careful excavation and the ground plan worked out. The walls of the buildings were of clay daub, which was shuttered on both sides while it was drying out and then combed before it was hard dry to give a key for the plaster that was applied inside and out. The roofs would have been either of wooden shingles or baked clay tiles (*tegulae*). In the time of the military base, wooden shingles were almost certainly used as no large roofing tiles have been found in the earliest levels. Roofs were pitched at a fairly shallow angle and were brought well out over the walls so as to shed the water away from them into eaves-drip gulleys and provide maximum protection from driving rain. Drainage of surface water must always have been a problem, but the military architects provided a system which took the water from the eaves-drip gulleys around the buildings into larger surface water drains, lined with timber, with wooden covers which could be removed for cleaning out the drains when they silted up (Pl. 9). In Chichester, which is a well drained site, the timber survives, as we have seen, only as stains in the clay, but the linings and revetments have survived on other Roman sites which have remained waterlogged until the present day, and from these the design can be worked out.

It is likely that much of the timberwork for the original legionary barracks was pre-fabricated, brought to site and erected by the army. In Chapel Street, below the Telephone Exchange, charred beams were found, slightly out of position, with pre-drilled holes at regular intervals along the length, suggesting that on the demolition of

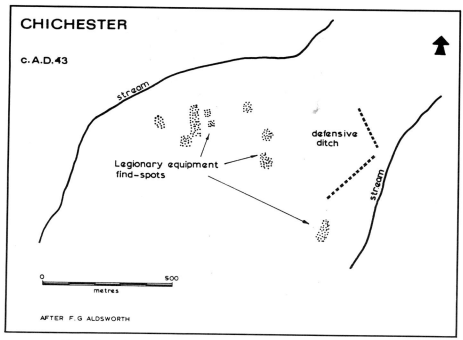

5. Map of the Chichester area showing find-spots of military equipment.

6. Plan of military timber buildings at Fishbourne (after B. W. Cunliffe).

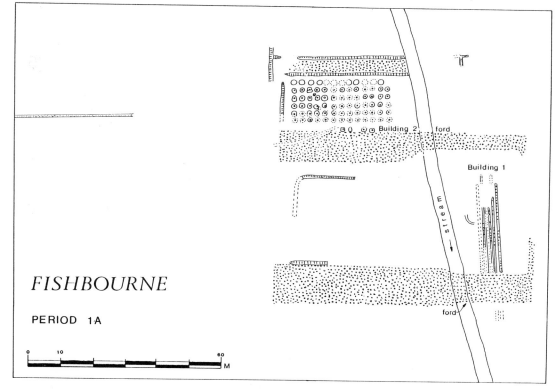

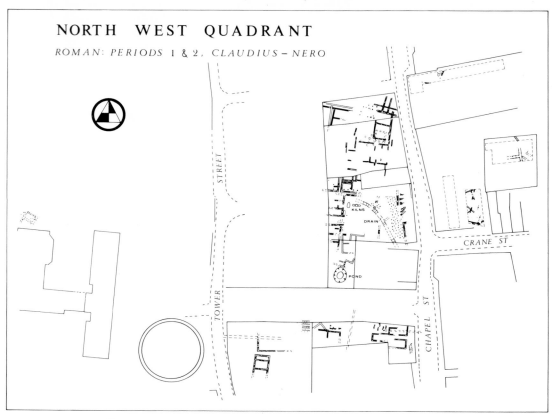

NORTH WEST QUADRANT

ROMAN: PERIODS 1 & 2, CLAUDIUS — NERO

7. Plan of the Chapel Street area showing military-style timber buildings.

8. Excavations at Chapel Street: Roman timber buildings below the Wool Store.

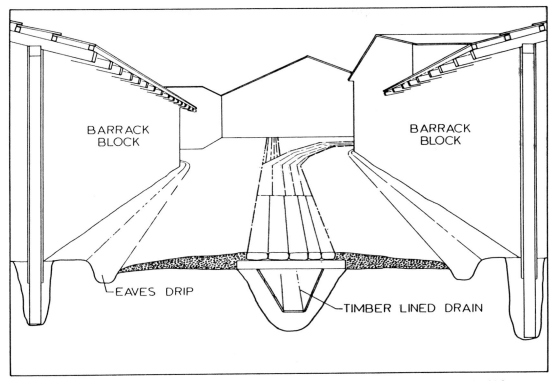

9.   Schematic drawing showing section across reconstructed legionary barrack block. (After Schonberger – Kastell Oberstimm, Germania.)

the building the sound timbers may have been salvaged and returned to stores and the unserviceable ones left to rot or burnt on site (Pl. 8). No floor levels could be positively identified with the military phase, possibly because the houses would have had planked floors which meant that little, if any, debris accumulated below them.

If floor levels were difficult to establish, the finds of armour and other equipment shed by the legionaries was prolific. Javelins (pilae), stabbing spears, ballista bolt-heads and a complete legionary *gladius* or short sword were found below the Central Girls' School in Chapel Street (now the Providence). The sword was found below a later building of Flavian date, lying in the mud where, judging by the grass impressions on the corrosion products on the blade, it may have been wrapped in a legionary's palliasse (Pls. 10 & 11). The gladius showed no signs of wear and might have been a spare blade from the armourer's store. On the other hand, it could have been carried and used against the Catuvellauni at the battle of the Medway a short time before it was lost.

In addition to the weaponry, many fragments of the segmented cuirass worn as body armour by the legionaries – the *lorica segmentata* – have been found on sites as far apart as County Hall in the north-west of the town and the Cattlemarket outside the Eastgate.

10. Roman gladius lying where it was found below a later Roman timber house.

11. Roman gladius from Chapel Street after conservation.

Various reconstructions have been made of this body armour, which was modified from time to time by the army, and there is a scale model of a legionary in the Chichester District Museum which gives an accurate representation of the equipment worn in the 1st and 2nd century A.D., based on armour found at Corbridge, the main supply base for Hadrian's Wall (Pl. 12). The surviving fragments of the overlapping segments of iron plate can usually be identified by X-Ray photography, when the bronze hinges which joined the various sections can be clearly seen where they are rivetted to the plates (Pl. 13).

The legionaries, in addition to being highly disciplined fighting men, were required to carry out civil engineering works, and digging ditches, building roads and constructing fortifications came second only to fighting. It was standard practice to surround the camp with a bank and ditch for defence at night and the bank would be surmounted by a palisade. So far, it has not been possible to identify with certainty the defences

12. Model of a legionary in the Chichester District Museum, wearing the equipment of the first century A.D.

13. X-ray photograph of a fragment of iron plate from the legionary cuirass, the *lorica segmentata*. Part of the bronze lobate hinge remains rivetted to the plate.

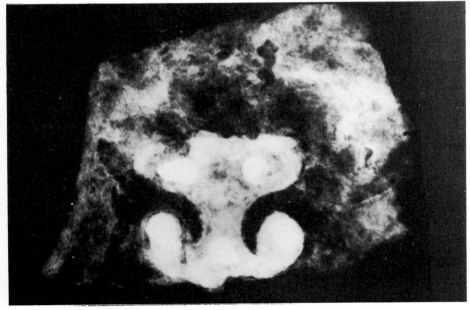

around the Second Legion's original camp, but a ditch of defensive proportions was found outside the Eastgate, below the Roman cemetery there. It was aligned north-south and was square-cut at the bottom (Pl. 14), and had not remained open very long after it was dug.[7] In 1978 another 'leg' of this defensive work was found when the Needlemakers site was excavated[8] and another section of the same ditch was found on the Cattlemarket site in 1982.[9] The two 'legs' projected towards one another suggest that a defensive perimeter existed on the east side of the later town (fig. 15) and that it probably extended below it. The dating evidence from the ditch silts and the relationship of the ditch to the Roman Stane Street indicates that this enclosure pre-dates the road and probably belongs to the earliest part of the Roman occupation. The likeliest explanation is that it *is* legionary in origin and may have been one of several enclosures constructed for the legion or the auxiliaries. A third ditch of similar size has recently been discovered outside the Westgate[10] and the finds associated with it show that the area was occupied by the military. This ditch, in view of the distance from the other two, must belong to another enclosure.

At Fishbourne, Professor Cunliffe's excavations have demonstrated that the earliest levels of activity were military and comprised storebuildings of a type found at the legionary base at Richborough, in Kent,[11] which was the main base for the invasion troops. He also found a number of items of military equipment, mostly as rubbish survivals in later levels, but it is clear that much of the evidence for the military port and storebuildings must lie beneath the Flavian palace. Recent excavations east of the palace in 1983 and 1985–6 in advance of the new A27 Fishbourne by-pass have uncovered post-pits belonging to a granary-type structure extending eastwards from the palace site and another series of large postholes further east still, on the line of the new road. These may also belong to the military phase, but their precise function is unclear.[12]

The dating evidence

In a consumer orientated society like the Roman, domestic pottery was mass-produced in a number of centres and the finer wares shipped to all quarters of the Empire, where it usually found a ready market. The troops who came to Britain with Aulus Plautius were well supplied with fine red-slipped wares from Italy and Gaul, known to us as 'samian' wares or *vasa samia*[13] as well as other fine pottery and a large range of wine containers – amphorae, jugs and flagons. Most of the manufacturing centres in Gaul and Italy are known and some of the pottery can be dated to within 10–25 years, thus giving the archaeologist studying this period a tremendous advantage. The earliest Roman pottery found in Chichester dates, not to the reign of Claudius, but to the later years of Augustus, and some of it is between 30–40 years old at the time of the invasion. The pottery, which includes Arretine ware from Arrezo in Italy and a limited range of Terra Nigra and Terra Rubra from Gaul, has so far only been found in the north-west quadrant, Westgate, Cattlemarket and Fishbourne; in other words, in areas where the military were.

It has been suggested that this 'early' pottery might be yet further proof of an Atrebatic *oppidum* in the vicinity which traded with Rome before the invasion and which, perhaps, had stocks for sale to the troops when they arrived. On the other hand, it might be that this old stock had been in the quartermaster's stores for a long

14.   Military defensive ditch below St Pancras Roman cemetery.

15.   Plan of defensive ditches on the east side of the Roman town.

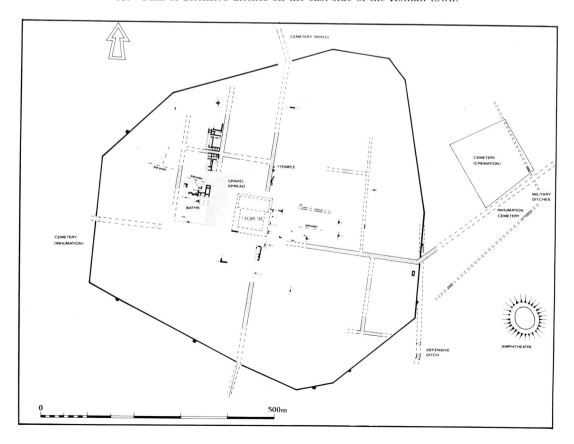

time and had been off-loaded on to the troops or perhaps even local traders. The silver Iron Age minims (see p. 1) can also be explained in the legionary occupation levels as evidence of trade with the natives. In the early years of the invasion there was a shortage of regular Roman coin issues and it is likely that the native coinage was used as 'small change' to supplement the Roman money. The local people would have been eager to trade with the troops and the speed with which the entrepreneurs set up shop around the military establishment (a phenomenon well attested in practically every military occupation before and since), must have been one of the reasons for the establishment of the later town on the same site.

By A.D. 44 or 45 the main body of the troops must have moved on and by A.D. 46 there may have been no more than a depot remaining, possibly in the Chapel Street area. They left behind military buildings, port installations and a lasting impression of the organisation and power that was Rome. For the local Atrebates, who were on the winning side, the future must have seemed bright. Although the military had gone (or almost gone), trade with Gaul was opening up still further; *negotiatores* were moving in and there were doubtless many opportunities for contracts to supply the army with goods and services. That these opportunities were fully exploited may have been largely due to the organising genius and enterprise of one man.

Chapter Two

Tiberius Claudius Cogidubnus

We first hear of King Cogidubnus from Tacitus (Agricola xiv) when, summarising the events in Britain before the arrival of his father-in-law Agricola as Governor in A.D. 78, he wrote '... certain civitates were given to Cogidubnus, he remained loyal down to our own times'. This has been taken to mean that Cogidubnus ruled as a client king under the Romans and that he was given other territories to govern in addition to his own kingdom because his loyalty could be relied upon. The practice of ruling indirectly through client kings (in much the same way as the British later ruled parts of India through local hereditary rulers) had much to recommend it from the Roman point of view, as it was economic in manpower, the natives continued to be governed by their own tribal aristocracy and received the benefits of the *pax Romana* at one remove from their conquerors. However, unlike the British in India, the sons of client kings under the Romans did not necessarily inherit and, on the death of a ruler, his lands were liable to be absorbed into the Roman administrative system, which was normally based on the tribal area.

Cogidubnus is also known from the inscription found in the city in 1723 (see below) and the splendid palace excavated by Professor Cunliffe at Fishbourne may well have been his residence. His origins are uncertain, but it seems most likely that he was a member of the Atrebatic ruling house, perhaps a son or nephew of Verica. His name, expressing his links with the Emperor Claudius, and the architectural style of the palace, suggests a thoroughly Romanised prince who knew Rome at first hand. He may have been sent there to complete his education, like so many other sons of tribal rulers friendly to Rome, and he may still have been there when Verica fled from Britain to ask for help against his enemies.

The young Cogidubnus may well have been brought back by the invaders and used to rally support in the south of Britain at the most critical point of the invasion. Alternatively he may have already been on the spot, organising resistance to the Catuvellauni when the invasion took place. Either way, he would have been acceptable both to Rome and the Atrebates, and would have been a natural choice as a successor to Verica at a time when the Roman army needed a stabilised region from which to operate. We do not know whether Verica ever came back to Britain after the event. If he was still alive in 43 he may well have been restored to his kingdom and Rome could thus be seen to demonstrate that she stood by her alliances. However, in view of his age and the fact that the situation called for a younger man, he is unlikely to have reigned for more than a year or so before either dying or abdicating in favour of Cogidubnus, whose succession would undoubtedly have been approved by Claudius. In the event, the choice of Cogidubnus was a signal success for the Romans, as can be seen by the laudatory passage in *Agricola* and the rapid development of his territory on Roman lines.

Cogidubnus is not known to have minted any coins, which seems to indicate that he did not rule before the Romans arrived, and the 'certain civitates' mentioned by

Tacitus as having been given to him to govern can only refer to lands peripheral to his own boundaries. The most likely are, perhaps, Kent (the Cantiaci) and the northern Atrebatic territory of which Silchester (Calleva Atrebatum) was the capital.

It must have been a tremendous advantage for the Roman General Staff to have a base in friendly territory from which to launch the attack on the south and west. There was no need for Vespasian to watch his back while he was assaulting the Isle of Wight and the consequent saving in manpower would have been very welcome. There would also have been an abundance of labour to construct the harbour facilities and ease the problems of transporting supplies. The army would require large amounts of agricultural products; corn, meat, hides and salt would have been the principal products of the coastal plain and hinterland, and could be secured with greater facility from a friendly population.

By A.D. 46 it is likely that the main body of troops would have gone, but by that time Cogidubnus had probably taken the decision to make his new capital, not at the old oppidum at Selsey, which might already have started to suffer from erosion from the sea, but at the site of the legionary base camp, which was already laid out on a plan and around which some of the local traders had already started to settle.

Apart from the reference to him in Tacitus and the inscription found in Lion Street, history is silent about his achievements, but a certain amount of information can be gleaned from the archaeological record. By A.D. 58, in the reign of Nero, public buildings were being erected in the town and industrial activity in the form of metal-working and pottery making was being carried on in the Chapel Street area on the site of the demolished barrack buildings.[1] On one site below the Central Girls School the timber buildings of the military had been replaced by more substantial buildings – still of timber-framed construction, but on dwarf walls of flint. At roughly the same time, enamelling of small bronze objects of jewellery was taking place nearby and an extensive range of fine pottery, imitating the sophisticated imports from Gaul, was being produced in kilns below the school, using Reading beds clay dug out from the shores of Chichester harbour (Pl. 16).

At Fishbourne, Professor Cunliffe found masonry buildings which pre-dated the Flavian palace and one of these, on the east side, was incorporated into the final plan of the later building. He identified this as the 'proto-palace' which he dated to the reign of Nero and it has been suggested that this was the king's earliest residence. In 1983, trial excavations in the field to the east of the palace uncovered another masonry structure on the same alignment as the east wing (Pl. 17). This had been destroyed and partly robbed and a road was laid across the demolished foundations, possibly at the same time as the great Flavian palace was being constructed. At the time of writing, the pottery evidence has not been closely examined by specialists, but the method of construction and the alignment of the building suggests that it may be of the same date as the 'proto-palace'.

On the site of the Roman public baths in Chichester, now largely covered by the Army and Navy Stores and the Telephone Exchange, the mass of building debris excavated in 1974–5 from the foundation trenches at the north end (opposite the Public Library), showed that the workmanship of some of the finer masonry details, together with fragments of inscriptions and imported marble from Italy and Greece, was very similar to that found by Professor Cunliffe at Fishbourne. The inference is inescapable.

16. Roman kiln in Chapel Street after re-firing.

17. Plan of Fishbourne Roman Palace.

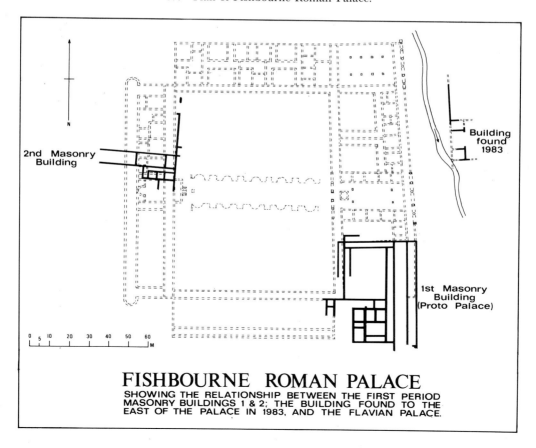

FISHBOURNE ROMAN PALACE

SHOWING THE RELATIONSHIP BETWEEN THE FIRST PERIOD
MASONRY BUILDINGS 1 & 2; THE BUILDING FOUND TO THE
EAST OF THE PALACE IN 1983, AND THE FLAVIAN PALACE.

At the same time, or shortly after the Flavian palace was constructed (probably between A.D. 75–90), the masons and other craftsmen moved into the new town and began work on the public baths. It is likely that their programme also included other public buildings in the town and, indeed, in other parts of the region. This intense period of building activity probably spanned three decades, from the late 50s to the late 80s. Where did the money come from? The resources required to build the palace and the new town would have been considerable, with the cost of imported craftsmen and materials figuring high on the list. It is unlikely that Cogidubnus received any cash hand-outs from Rome, but the army would have been a good customer for the Wealden iron which lay wihin the king's territory, as well as the agricultural products mentioned earlier. In the early years, Cogidubnus would have had control of one of the principal supply ports to Britain and there would have been a heavy flow of goods from Italy and Gaul, shipped over by entrepreneurs anxious to exploit the new market opened up for them by the legions. It could not fail to offer opportunities for enrichment to the local traders, from whom, no doubt, the king took his share. There is the evidence from the Cogidubnus inscription (see p.22) that by the 60s the king had permitted the organisation of at least one guild of craftsmen who were wealthy enough to build and dedicate a temple to Neptune and Minerva, and this is yet another pointer to an expanding region able to afford some of the benefits of Romanised life at a very early stage in the life of the new province.

But whether these factors were enough to account for all the early development is doubtful. It might well be, as E. W. Black suggests, that some Atrebatic nobles borrowed heavily from Gallic moneylenders at high rates of interest, to finance their luxurious new villas and, as a result, interest payments on the loans would have become a heavy burden to succeeding generations which might eventually be impossible to sustain.

Outside the area of the town, but within Sussex, we know of four villas with 'early' characteristics, which seem to have their origins at about the same time as the proto-palace was being built at Fishbourne, late in Nero's reign. Professor Cunliffe has suggested that they might represent the estates of some of the wealthy Atrebatic aristocracy,[2] but unfortunately, apart from the proto-palace, none of the villas has been excavated under modern conditions, so the full story of their development and decline has not been traced. At the Angmering villa,[3] the bath-house has close architectural affinities with the baths in the proto-palace at Fishbourne. The villa at Southwick[4] appears to have been constructed in the late 1st century and, again, the design and layout of the rooms is similar to the Flavian palace. Much the same can be said about the villa excavated at Borough Farm, Pulborough in 1907–8[5] and the fourth villa, at Eastbourne, has similar hypocaust tiles to those used at Fishbourne and Angmering and these can be dated to the time of Nero. Unfortunately, part of the Eastbourne villa is below a housing estate and some has been eroded by the sea. The evidence is scrappy and inconclusive, but it does point to the development of sophisticated masonry villas in Sussex in the late 1st century A.D. which must reflect the early development of Romanisation in Cogidubnus's kingdom, due to the unique circumstances. Without stretching the historical and archaeological evidence too far, it seems likely that, after the Second Legion left the Chichester/Fishbourne region c. A.D. 45–46, the area developed under the rule of Cogidubnus, with the old military port installations being converted to civilian use and the site of the legionary base as the new capital. The full industrial potential seems to have developed at some speed, with the mineral and agricultural resources of the Weald and coastal plain making a large contribution to the wealth of the Atrebatic ruler and his nobles. With additional territory given to him to govern for the Romans and a positive Romanising policy to carry out, Cogidubnus emerges as a remarkable character of great energy and determination.

We do not know the full extent of his town and only large scale excavation in other parts of Chichester on the same scale as that carried out in the north-west quadrant would enable archaeologists to attempt the task of establishing the boundaries. Certainly, the industrial activity in Chapel Street dates to the reign of Nero as does the earliest part of the public baths in Tower Street. To this can be added the temple of Neptune and Minerva at the junction of Lion Street with North Street; the timber-framed houses below the Central Girls School in Chapel Street and, perhaps, some of the earlier phases of timber buildings on the Cattlemarket site. The town was probably a sprawling affair, with numbers of squalid timber buildings (some laid out in straight lines) and a few impressive masonry structures.

The public baths and the temple of Neptune and Minerva have been mentioned and their location is now known or can be inferred. A third large building may possibly

18.   The Cogidubnus inscription outside the Council House in North Street.

belong to Cogidubnus's time. In 1740 a dedicatory inscription was found at the corner of East Street and St. Martin's Street which may have come either from a public building or possibly an Imperial statue. It was lost soon after it was found, but luckily the inscription was recorded and it is dated to A.D. 58–60. It reads:

> NERONI CLAUDIO DIVI (CLAUDI FG)ERMANI (CI CAES N) EPOTI
> TI (CAES P) RONEPOTI DIV(I) (AVG ABNEPOTI) CAESARI AVG (I)
> R P IV IMP COS C V C

'To Nero Claudius, son of the Divine Claudius, grandson of Germanicus Caesar, great grandson of Tiberius Caesar, great-great grandson of the Divine Augustus Caesar, Augustus with Tribunician power for the fourth time, Consul for the fourth time'

During recent years, street works have shown that there is a large building below the shops and offices along the north side of East Street and a massive wall running northwards below St. Martin's Street near to the place where the inscription was found. It is likely that the inscription relates to this building, but it would require the demolition of all the modern buildings on the site to prove the point.

The Cogidubnus inscription is one of the most famous in Britain and was found in 1723 at the corner of North Street and Lion Street, when a cellar was being dug (Pl. 18).

The stone is of Purbeck marble and the left-hand portion is missing. It was broken into four pieces during recovery and has been joined together with cement, not very skilfully. The stone was acquired by the then Duke of Richmond and restored at Goodwood, where it was kept for some years. It is now mounted on the wall outside the Council House in North Street, only a few yards from where it was found. As recorded in RIB 91, the text reads:

> (N) EPTUNO ET MINERVAE
>   TEMPLUM
> (PR)O SALUTE DO(MUS) DIVINAE
> (EX) AVCTORITAT(E) TI (BERI) CLAUD (I)
> (CO)GIDUBNI R(EGIS) LEGA(TI) AVG(USTI) IN BRIT(ANNIA)
> (COLLE)GIUM FABROR(UM) ET (Q)UI IN EO
> (SUN)T D(E) S(UO) D(EDERENT) DONANTE AREAM
>   ...ENTE PVDENTINI FIL

'To Neptune and Minerva, for the welfare of the Divine House by the authority of Tiberius Claudius Cogidubnus, King, Imperial Legate in Britain, the guild of smiths [or shipwrights] and those therein gave this temple from their own resources, ...ens, son of Pudentinus, presenting the site.' The fifth line of this inscription has always presented historians and archaeologists with a problem. As interpreted, it gives Cogidubnus the title of *legatus augusti* (imperial legate) in Britain, an unheard of title for a client king. It would make Cogidubnus unique in Roman history, and for many years a number of theories have been put forward to account for this honour. His support of the Romans during the invasion period, his loyalty to them at the time of the Boudican revolt, or possibly his support of Vespasian's candidature when he became Emperor, have all been canvassed as possible reasons for granting him the title, but Professor Bogaers of Nijmegan University has now re-examined the inscription. He points out that the text as given in RIB 91 derives from a reading of the fifth line by the antiquary Roger Gale in September 1723, whereas a previous drawing of it by Dr Edward Bayly, Rector of Havant, shows the critical part of line 5 as 'AGN BRIT' instead of AVGN BRIT. If Dr Bayly's drawing is accepted, then Cogidubnus becomes *'rex magnus Brit'* (great King in Britain) instead of *legatvs augusti* and the need to find an explanation for a unique honour granted to a client king ceases to exist.[6]

A third inscription which might date to Cogidubnus's era has recently been found outside the Eastgate on the Needlemakers site. It was found in a pit cut into the top of the Roman legionary ditch and only a few fragments survive. It is now in the Chichester District Museum (Pl. 19). It probably came from a shrine dedicated to the *Matres Domesticae* and reads:

MATRI] BVS DOMEST/ [...]VS ARK/ [DS]P

Matri]bus Domest[icis/ [...]us ark(arius)/ [d(e) s (uo) p(osuit)

'To the Mother Goddesses of the Homeland .....the treasurer set this up at his own expense.'

19.   The inscription from Eastgate Needlemakers.

The unknown arkarius, or treasurer, who built the shrine could have been an important municipal official attached to a guild or else some important household, possibly even that of Cogidubnus.[7]

Cogidubnus may have lived on into the last quarter of the 1st century. Professor Cunliffe dates the Flavian palace at Fishbourne to c. A.D. 75 and by then Cogidubnus, if he still lived, would have been well advanced in years. In estimating his lifespan it is necessary to make some assumptions about his age at the time of the invasion. It is likely that he was a mature man in A.D.43 and his subsequent career suggests that he was no youthful puppet whom the Romans could manipulate or ignore. If we assume that he was about 25 years old in A.D. 43 he would have been 57 in A.D. 75 – a good age for those days. By A.D. 80 he would have been in his early 60s and it is possible that he might have died within five years either side of that date. Much depends on whether the Flavian palace was constructed in his time, or whether, as has recently been suggested, the proto-palace was the king's only residence and the Flavian palace was built by his heirs.[8] This would imply that Cogidubnus died or abdicated at some time in the 60s. The reference to him by Tacitus (Agricola xiv) implies that he had remained faithful to the Romans 'down to his own memory'. Tacitus was writing in AD 97/98 and the phrase he used is ambiguous. Much would depend on how old he was at the time of writing and how far back he was remembering.

With Cogidubnus's death came a change in the character of the town. Roman policy in the Flavian period tended to view client kingdoms with disfavour and was inclined to replace them with direct rule. Accordingly, upon his death his territory was absorbed into the Roman administrative system. His southern capital *Noviomagus* became the civitas capital of the southern Atrebates, or *Regni* as they were now called. The new region probably covered all of Sussex and part of eastern Hampshire, with Silchester (*Calleva Atrebatum*) becoming the regional capital of the northern part of the old Atrebatic territory and Winchester (*Venta Belgarum*) the cantonal capital of the Belgae.

The incorporation of the client kingdom into the Roman province would require careful and delicate handling, and the three newly formed *civitates* would need help and guidance in establishing a form of local self-rule on the Roman model. In the last 20 years of the first century, two distinguished lawyers are known to have been in Britain. *C.Salvius Liberalis* was an advocate well thought of by Vespasian, and he was likely to have been in Britain c.80–81, whilst *J. Javolenus Priscus* a well known and respected writer on Roman law, was known to have been here between A.D. 84–86. Agricola was the Governor at the time and both these jurors may have been attached to his staff to advise him on the complex legal problems involved.

It is possible that Cogidubnus may have constructed defences for his town at some time in the third quarter of the 1st century. Excavations at the Cattlemarket site uncovered a large defensive ditch over 7 metres wide and 2.5 metres deep, running northwards towards the Eastgate.[9] It runs at an acute angle below the city wall north of the Eastgate (Pl. 20) and must therefore pre-date the defences, which are of the late 2nd century (see Chapter 3) It is considerably wider than the legionary defences on the east side of the town. (Pl. 21). Only a short length of the ditch has been uncovered at present and there are several possibilities which can be canvassed. It is roughly in line with the most westerly of two of the Chichester Entrenchments which run southwards from the Broyle (Pl. 22). This ditch has not been traced as far as the town and

20. Earlier defensive works at Chichester and
Silchester.

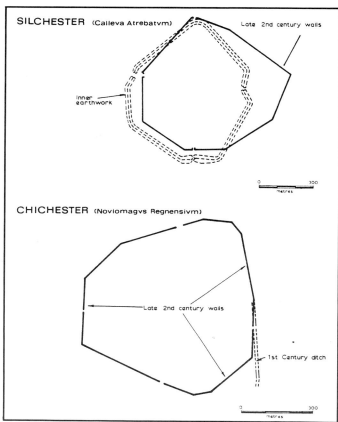

SILCHESTER (Calleva Atrebatvm)

Late 2nd century walls

Inner
earthwork

0   300
metres

CHICHESTER (Noviomagvs Regnensivm)

Late 2nd century walls

1st Century ditch

0   300
metres

21. The first-century defensive ditch in the
Cattlemarket.

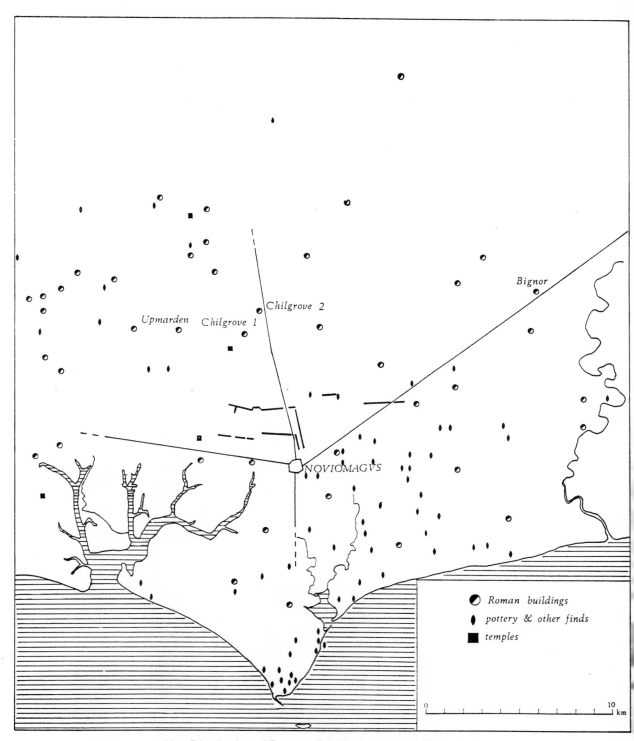

Bignor

Chilgrove 2

Upmarden   Chilgrove 1

NOVIOMAGVS

⬤ Roman buildings
◆ pottery & other finds
■ temples

0   10
⊢─┴─┴─┴─┴─┴─┴─┴─┴─┴─┤ km

22.   Distribution of Romano-British sites around Chichester.

has never been sectioned, but the one to the east, which runs parallel to it and goes through the grounds of Graylingwell Hospital, has been sectioned. It is likely that these two ditches have their origin in the Iron Age and are roughly of the same date, i.e. mid-late 1st century B.C. The recorded section across the Graylingwell ditch shows that it is not as large as the Cattlemarket one and the profile is different. It is possible that the Cattlemarket ditch was constructed as a defence around the legionary base camp shortly after the legion arrived and possibly in A.D. 44. If this was so, then it would have been a more permanent defence, unlike the 'marching camp' ditches on the east and west sides of the later town, which would have been dug as a temporary measure on arrival. As the Cattlemarket ditch manifestly encloses a different area from that of the later town the possibility that it was constructed by Cogidubnus when he established his native town on the site must also be considered. He might, in fact, have adapted any legionary defensive work already there, especially if he was faced wih an emergency such as the Boudican revolt of A.D.59–60. At *Calleva* (Silchester), where Cogidubnus may also have ruled under the Romans, there is, partly below the later 2nd–century defences, a defensive ditch known as the Inner Earthwork (Pl. 20). This ditch, like the Cattlemarket one, enclosed a different area from that of the later town, and the most recent thinking on the subject[10] indicates that it was probably constructed in the 1st century B.C., although George Boon has been able to show that parts of it were not completely backfilled until after A.D. 60. He has suggested that it might have been constructed by Cogidubnus as a defence during the troubles of A.D. 47–48 when Caractacus was actively campaigning against the Romans but, if Fulford is right and the Inner Earthwork is earlier, then it was still available to fulfill a defensive function during the Cogidubnian era. *Calleva's* geographical position meant that there could have been two threats to the town – the first during 47–48 and the second in 59–60. Chichester, on the other hand, would have been threatened only by the Boudican revolt. There would have been no time to dig fresh defences. Boudica could have been at Chichester within a matter of a few weeks after burning London and if, as has recently been suggested, the revolt had spread to the Durotriges in Dorset, then the Regni would have had hostile forces to the north and west. In those circumstances, Cogidubnus might have had three choices open to him. To cut and run; to join the insurgents; or to dig in and prepare to fight. The laudatory passage in Tacitus indicates that he chose the last option.

Possibly the best explanation of the Cattlemarket ditch is that it might be a legionary adaptation of an original Iron Age defence and that it was maintained by Cogidubnus at least up to A.D. 60, when that part of it which runs through the Cattlemarket was backfilled. The part of the Inner Earthwork at Silchester examined by Boon seems to have been backfilled at about the same time, but whether it is coincidence or whether the slighting of the defences of both Atrebatic towns indicates a change of status (perhaps due to the death of Cogidubnus) we do not know. Much more of the Cattlemarket ditch needs to be traced and excavated before we can be sure about the date of the backfilling, as although the sample of pottery found during the excavations was quite large, other sections along its length might tell a different story.

Chapter Three

The Development of the Roman Town

The Roman name for Chichester was *Noviomagus Regnensium*. The town was referred to as *Regno* in the Antonine Itinerary and as *Noviomago Regentium* in the Ravenna Cosmography. *Noviomagus* can be interpreted as 'the new market or town' but there is more than one meaning for the rest of the name. Ptolemy calls the people *Regni*, and if the word derives from the Latin *Regnum* (kingdom), then it could mean 'the new town (market) of the people of the kingdom'. Another suggestion is that the word *Regni* comes from the Celtic word *Regini*, meaning 'the proud ones, the stiff ones'. If this is correct, then *Noviomagus Reginorum* may be the right name, meaning 'the new town (or market) of the proud people.'

Upon the establishment of the town as a *civitas* capital after the death of Cogidubnus, a certain amount of re-planning may have been necessary. The new status would require a forum and basilica and the town would have been laid out with a properly planned street grid. Some of the town planning had already been done by the military and it is no coincidence that the alignment of the later Roman streets follows that of the earlier timber buildings laid out by the Second Legion. It is also possible that military surveyors and architects were available to assist in the planning of the new regional capital of the Regni as part of Agricola's policy of encouraging the development of the Roman way of life.

Assuming that Cogidubnus must have died somewhere between A.D. 70 and 85, it is at some time after that date that we might expect to see evidence for the re-planning of the town. Excavations carried out in the North-West quadrant in the Chapel Street and Tower Street sites between 1969 and 1974, added to evidence from earlier digs and observation of street works, have shown that the earliest buildings of first-century date were covered by a large gravel spread which extends southwards towards the centre of the town (Pl. 23). The latest pottery found below it is of second century Antonine date. For the first two centuries A.D. the glossy red samian ware (*vasa samia*) manufactured in Gaul is the most reliable dating evidence available to us. It tells a remarkably consistent story in this instance, as four areas have yielded the same result; below the old Wool Store (now the Telephone Exchange) and below Crane Street, North Street and West Street. The Roman street below Chapel Street where a large area was excavated gives a slightly earlier date, which might indicate that it had originally been laid out by the military, or perhaps during the time of the old king in the last quarter of the first century.

While the spread of gravel, which varied in thickness from half a metre to a metre, sealed only timber buildings in the Chapel Street area, street works in front of the Dolphin and Anchor in West Street in 1977[1] showed the gravel lying above a mass of demolished building debris which included greensand ashlar masonry, painted wall plaster and roof tiles. It was in the dirty clay below these deposits that the second-century samian was found. The impression gained is that there was certainly a large landscaping operation carried out in the centre of the town and that some buildings were demolished or already in ruins when it was done. The hint of an earlier date for at least one of the streets could mean that the re-planning of the town on formal lines was carried out on an *ad hoc* basis and, in view of the presence of the Antonine samian, at a fairly leisurely pace. Probably some of the streets came first, with the landscaping of the central area being achieved as and when buildings were ripe for development and when funds allowed. The evidence of the pottery, whilst not conclusive, suggests that this re-modelling of the central area was still going on in the mid to late second century. If it is assumed that the operation originally started soon after Cogidubnus died, then a period of about 60–70 years elapsed before the centre of the town was finally finished. This seems a very long time, and we may in fact be looking at a development which did not start until the early second century. Only a study of a larger sample of pottery excavated from below the gravel over a wide area could give a firm pointer. So far, we have four areas yielding Antonine samian but we should be cautious about coming to general conclusions on the basis of such a small sample, especially as only two of the sites were archaeologically excavated.

All the earlier buildings, both civil and military, were built of timber and clay, and the regular demolition and replacement of these wattle and daub structures in the central area of the town gave a soil rise of between 25 to 40cms from the time the first buildings were placed there c.A.D. 43–44 until the last were demolished in the second century. Each time a hut was knocked down, the clay from the walls was spread and the post sockets for the next building were dug through it. Sometimes, when buildings were cleared from a site the sound posts were 'rocked' out of the ground, leaving oval-shaped post voids behind. The wattle hurdles supporting the walls were usually left to rot, leaving readily detectable stains in the clay. These timber buildings are not difficult to identify and the chronological sequence in which they were erected can usually be worked out, but dating them is another matter. Few identifiable floor levels can be established as many of the houses had planked floors and relating horizons to postholes is not always so easy.

All we can say is that we know the earliest horizon, which is the turf which grew on the site in A.D. 43 when the Second Legion arrived, and we know that between then and the time when the streets and the gravel spread was laid out was unlikely to have been less than about 40–45 years, allowing Cogidubnus to have died between A.D. 70–85, and likely to be more than a century if it is assumed that an Antonine date for the pottery means somewhere in the mid-Antonine period, say c. A.D. 150. During the period that the *civitas* capital was developing out of the native town, the public buildings grouped around the Forum would have been constructed. Little is known of these, except for fragments found below the streets and pavements during street works, but it is obvious from what remains that the standard of building was very high, as might be expected. The foundations of the buildings below North Street are massive and those below East Street, the north end of South Street and the north side of West Street in front of the Dolphin and Anchor are to a similar high specification (Pl. 23).

Roman Government

Noviomagus Regnensium, as a *civitas peregrina*, would have been governed by a Council or *ordo*, which was independent in local affairs and consisted of 100 decurions or

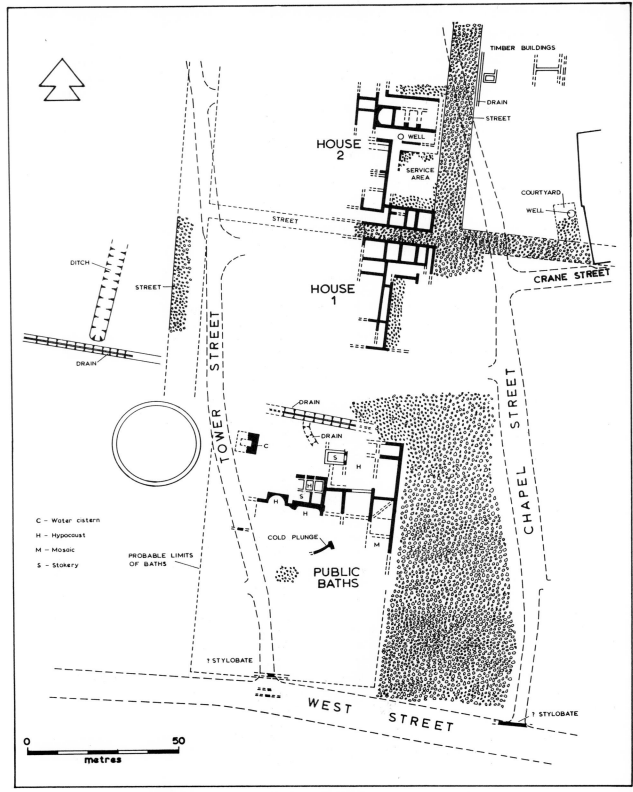

TIMBER BUILDINGS

DRAIN

STREET

HOUSE 2

WELL

SERVICE AREA

COURTYARD

WELL

CRANE STREET

STREET

DITCH

STREET

HOUSE 1

DRAIN

TOWER STREET

CHAPEL STREET

DRAIN

DRAIN

C

S

H

H

S

H

H

COLD PLUNGE

M

C – Water cistern
H – Hypocaust
M – Mosaic
S – Stokery

PROBABLE LIMITS OF BATHS

PUBLIC BATHS

? STYLOBATE

? STYLOBATE

WEST STREET

0   50
metres

23.   Fourth-century Roman features in the North-West Quadrant.

councillors. Its duties may be roughly equated with those functions which today are carried out by County and District Councils. Membership of the *ordo* was governed by a property qualification. The executive officers or magistrates were elected to office annually; an expensive business when it is realised that not only did they probably have to pay to be elected but, when in office, were expected to pay for games and public spectacles and to make public benefactions for the good of the town. Thus, only the rich nobles of the tribe would have been eligible for the honour of holding office, which might carry with it the grant of Roman citizenship when the period of service had ended. Celtic society, unlike the Roman, was country-based, with the aristocrats preferring to live on their estates rather than in the town, and some adjustments in outlook were necessary when the tribal area of the Regni was established, with the new town as the focus of local power.

Two pairs of magistrates were elected each year. The two *Duoviri iuridicundo* sat to hear all legal cases except the most important criminal and civil ones, which went to the Governor's court. Their functions might equate to the duties of the Magistrates and Crown Courts of our day. The *Duoviri aediles* were responsible for public works and the collection of taxes. As time went on, the responsibilities of office became more and more onerous and expensive and it became difficult to obtain volunteers for the posts, especially after Roman citizenship was extended to all citizens in the Empire, thus effectively removing one of the main incentives to undertake the burdens of public life.

The *ordo* met in a chamber in the basilica, which flanked one side of the forum, and it was here that local justice was administered and the collection of taxes and maintenance of public services was organised. The forum served as the main focus of civil life and followed a fairly standardised plan, although *fora* varied in size according to the wealth and importance of the town. The forum court (see Pl. 15) served as a market place, with the basilica at one end (usually the north), and the three other sides were occupied by shops and offices. At Silchester, a portico ran along three sides of the court and there were others outside the forum-basilica complex. Silchester is the nearest Roman town to Chichester where the complete plan of both forum and town is known and, since it may well have been of equal rank when it was part of Cogidubnus's kingdom, its subsequent status as a *civitas* capital is likely to have been equal to that of Chichester. Its forum probably dates from the same time, and it is a reasonable assumption that, in the first instance, the public buildings would have been of comparable size.

At Silchester, the forum-basilica complex measured roughly 90 by 99 metres, with the central court being 41 by 47 metres. The whereabouts of the forum in Chichester has not yet been established beyond all doubt but, following the tremendous upheavals in the city centre between 1979 and 1981 when the pedestrian precinct was being built, it is now possible to indulge in some informed guesswork. It has long been known that a large east-west masonry wall is present at the south end of the cellars in the Dolphin and Anchor which run below the pavement on the north side of West Street. Works by Southern Gas in 1981 showed that a large stylobate and gutter, aligned east-west, lies below the road, and the same street works revealed that there were several large paving slabs set in pink mortar at the junction of Chapel Street with West Street (Pl. 24 & 25). These discoveries add up to the presence of a large building below the

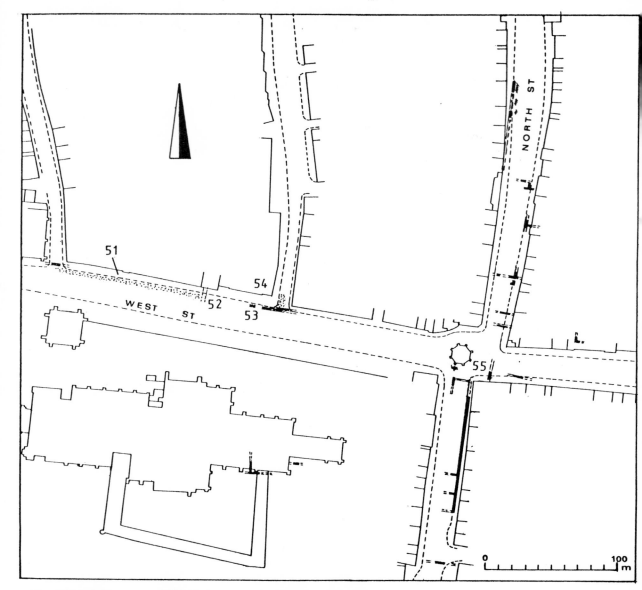

24. Map of the centre of Chichester, showing Roman masonry walls near the Forum area, discovered during street works.

Dolphin and Anchor which had a south-facing colonnade with a gutter alongside it and another colonnade along the west side, running northwards roughly on the line of Chapel Street. The portico between the colonnade and the main building was paved with substantial slabs of sandstone of the same size as those found at Fishbourne Roman palace. The artist's reconstruction (Pl. 25), which is partly based on the forum

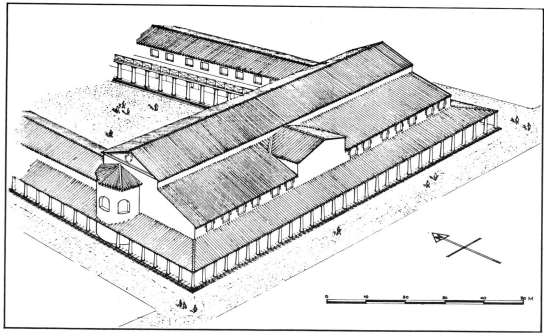

25a.   Conjectural reconstruction of the south end of the
Forum (after Silchester), by Max Wholey.

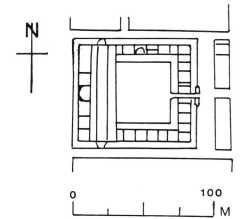

25b.   Silchester, Forum plan.

at Silchester, shows what this might have looked like. Another large building with
underfloor heating in at least one room is known to lie under the south end of North
Street, and this appears to be on a north-south alignment. If the measurements are
compared with the Silchester forum it can be seen that there is a strong possibility
that the forum complex in Chichester is within the rectangle formed by the building
below the north side of West Street and the one below North Street. The western
boundary might well be the large gravelled area mentioned above, with the public
baths (which are below the Army and Navy Stores and the Telephone Exchange) lying
on the west side of the open gravelled area. Nothing is known about the north end of

the presumed forum site, but if this suggestion is the right one, there should be another range of buildings (possibly the basilica) somewhere south of Crane Street.

When the foundations for the original Post Office were dug along the west side of the Chapel Street frontage in 1935, a statue base dedicated to Jupiter was found (Pl. 26).[2] This is precisely the kind of monument that could be expected around a forum precinct, and there should be others. The inscription was dated to the late second or early third century by Professor Collingwood[3] but Dr. Henig[4] has re-dated it to the first century both on the style of the lettering and the sculpture. It would seem more likely that it was erected during the early Flavian period at a time when the town was in its early stages of development. The stone is now in the Guildhall Museum in Priory Park. Finds of this nature, especially if they can be seen to be in their original position, are of special value to archaeologists, which is why they spend so much time looking into holes dug by other people.

At the north end of South Street and on the east side of it is a massive masonry wall running north-south (Pl. 24). It is nearly a metre wide and appears to be the eastern boundary wall of a building running westwards across the road towards the Cathedral. A substantially built house (possibly a public building) is known to lie below the Cathedral, and a very fine polychrome mosaic (Pl. 27) and fragments of Roman walls were found during underpinning operations between 1966–68.[5] These discoveries, added to earlier ones made in the 19th century when vaults were being constructed. are firm pointers to a major structure or structures extending westwards from South Street, at least as far as the Bell Tower. The function can only be conjectured, but it lies directly south of the public baths and might have been either another public building or perhaps the town house of a wealthy member of the *ordo*.

By the late second century A.D. the centre of the town had probably developed to its maximum, with the landscaping of the open areas more or less completed, the major public buildings erected and other large town houses built on the best sites. With the exception of part of the public baths it has not been possible to excavate any of these buildings and we have to rely on *ad hoc* observations coupled with old accounts of previous discoveries. Consequently, while fragmentary plans can be built up we cannot ascertain how often houses were re-built and altered; how they relate to other features, or where they fit into the time-scale. We do not know, for example, how often the forum was re-built and whether it was moved from one site to another, as has happened elsewhere. All we can do is to plot each fragment of wall as it appears and try to make a coherent pattern. The map (Pl. 15) shows the present state of our knowledge and the reader can see the difference between the north-west quadrant of the town where extensive development was preceded by large-scale excavation, and the remainder of the town plan, which reflects many years of patient observation of building sites and street works.

Whilst the important public buildings in the town were masonry built with very substantial foundations, the same does not hold good for the majority of the houses, which were of timber-framed construction on dwarf walls of flint or gravel, with wattle and daub infill, identical to those built a century earlier. Some interior partition walls were also built of clay, but usually little of this survived when the houses were demolished. Occasionally, as in House 2 in Chapel Street, the bottom few inches of a wall are preserved intact when the rest of the partition slumped over it. At Chapel Street,

26. Jupiter statue base from Chapel Street.

27. Polychrome mosaic floor beneath Chichester Cathedral. Probably second-century date. (Photograph of a drawing by D. S. Neal.)

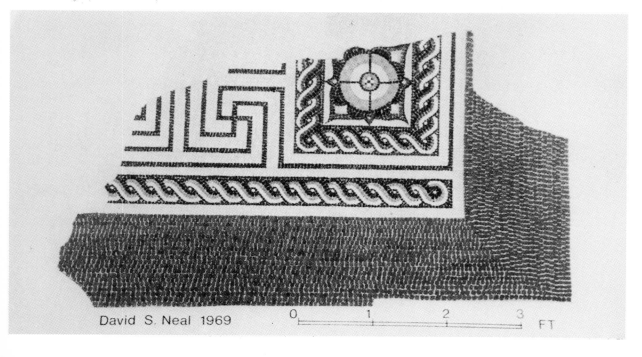

David S. Neal 1969

it could be seen that the wall was about 13 centimetres wide and the surface on both sides had been combed to provide a 'key' for the plaster, which was applied to a thickness of about 4.5 centimetres. Both faces of the plaster were then painted in bright colours (Pompeian red, yellow, blue and green).

28. Chapel Street Excavations. Base of a clay partition wall belonging to the Period 5 house north of the crossroads and dating to late third/early fourth century.

During the fourth century this same house was re-built and enlarged. It was reconstructed with substantial foundations in excess of 1.4 metres wide, with the walls above ground being 0.9 metre wide and solidly constructed of flint. With foundations of that size the house must have been masonry-built up to the eaves, and may have even been two storeys in height. Since the Norman Conquest the south-west quadrant of the town has been dominated by the cathedral and the religious precincts associated with it. As a result, little or no development has taken place in recent years and so very little is known of the Roman features which survive below the houses and gardens, although a mosaic or tessellated pavement is known in the garden in front of the Bishop's Palace,[6] and other fragments have been recorded below the Residentiary. The line of Canon Lane is in about the right place to be a Roman east-west street.

Mosaics

The fragment of polychrome mosaic found below the cathedral was thought by the excavator to be second century in date as it sealed a layer containing second-century pottery. The floor could, of course, be considerably later than the date of the pottery below it, but the substantial construction may be a pointer to the date suggested by the excavator. Below the Army and Navy Stores in West Street and opposite the cathedral, the fragment of geometric mosaic found during building operations in 1960 (Pl. 29) may well belong to the earliest phase of the public baths and could be contemporary with some of the Period 2 mosaics at Fishbourne, which it resembles (Pls. 30a & b). This would indicate a date of c. late first century for its construction. Elsewhere in the town, only one other significant fragment of mosaic has been recorded *in situ*. This is the floor discovered in 1959 behind David Greig's shop in East Street (now Mothercare).[7] It is very probably of fourth-century date and is

29.   Fragment of a geometric mosaic found below Morants in West Street (now Army and Navy Stores). The mosaic belongs to the Public Baths and is likely to be first century in date.

30a & b.   Two black and white geometric mosaics from Fishbourne Roman Palace, dating to the late first century. (a) Second Period mosaic in Room N12. (b) Second Period mosaic in Room N3.

now in the Guildhall Museum in Priory Park (Pl. 31). Fragments from a very fine polychrome mosaic were found in later cess-pits on the site of House 2 in Chapel Street in 1974 and 1977, but unfortunately no pieces survived in position. The dating evidence from below the floor levels indicates a fourth-century construction. At the time of writing (1987) a small fragment of mosaic is being excavated near the site of the old church of St. Peter-the-Less in North Street. The floor belongs to the same building first noted in 1959,[8] of which part was excavated by the writer in 1984 (Pl. 32).[9]

The full extent of the early *civitas* capital is not known, but it is certain that it occupied a larger area than that enclosed by the walls, which were probably erected towards the end of the second century. Part of the earlier town has been traced outside the West, North and East gates, but the position is complicated by the fact that suburbs eventually grew up alongside the roads issuing from the gates and it is difficult to disentangle the first-century occupation from the urban sprawl along the main roads in the succeeding centuries.

Suburbs have been traced outside the North, East and South gates, with the one outside the East gate being the most important. A cemetery occupied the land on the north side of Stane Street where it issued from Eastgate, but there is plenty of evidence from the south side of domestic occupation dating from the first century to the fourth, whilst on the present Cattlemarket site, south of the Hornet, recent excavations have shown that there was extensive occupation from the late first century to the early fifth. The area may well have been the tax collection point for the region for part of the time, as there is archaeological evidence for a whole range of activities including the storage of grain, grinding of corn and stockading of cattle and sheep. Fossilised insects recovered from a well included grain, flour and dung beetles in large numbers,[10] and many domestic cess-pits contained rich assemblages of fine pottery and glass – an indication that the artisans who were living and working there were reasonably prosperous. Scavenging dogs were much in evidence and numbers were found thrown into cess-pits, presumably during tidying-up operations. Some dog skeletons showed signs of mistreatment and many did not live beyond 18–24 months (Pl. 33). The latest activity during the late third to early fifth-century on this site appears to have been iron-working.

Outside the North gate, below Metropolitan House and the Fire Station, traces of timber and masonry buildings were found, associated with pottery of fourth-century date. This information was derived from observation on the foundation trenches during building operations and is not as reliable as evidence from properly stratified excavations. All it might indicate is the date when the suburb was last occupied. The area covered by buildings outside the North gate is likely to have been small and was probably confined to houses on both sides of the road to Silchester, which issued from the North gate. Trial excavations further north, across the area covered by the demolished suburb of Somerstown in 1965,[11] did not reveal any Roman structures and it is likely that the northern boundary of the Roman suburb was just south of St. Paul's church.

Outside the South gate there was domestic occupation on the land to the south of the modern railway. Excavations in 1975–6 revealed timber structures, a ditch and pits containing pottery and other finds, with a date range from the second to possibly the early fifth century.[12] Nearer to the town walls, a number of pits containing iron

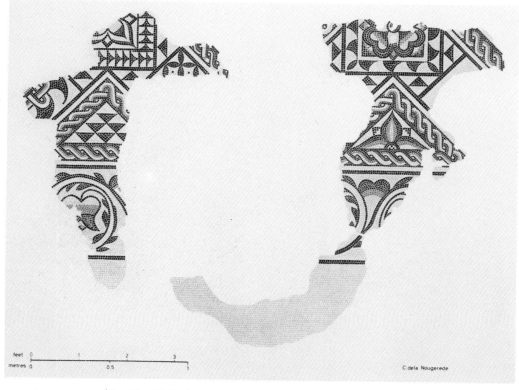

31. David Greig mosaic (drawing by C. de la Nougerede).

32. Fragment of polychrome mosaic from St Peter's, North Street, now in Fishbourne Roman Palace (drawn by D. J. Rudkin).

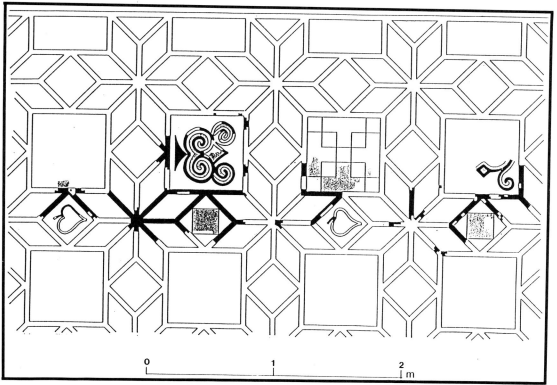

33.   Dead dog in the Cattlemarket.

slag were found during observation on building sites. The slag was from forging operations and points to the existence of a Roman smithy nearby.[13] Iron slag from forges has been found outside the East and West gates in the past and it seems that just outside the town was considered to be the best place for 'hot' industrial processes, which would represent a fire risk in a town where most of the houses were of timber. Not only that, but travellers leaving and entering Chichester would find it most convenient to have their horses re-shod at these points.

Apart from evidence for a forge, there is so far no trace of a suburb outside Westgate. Extensive trial trenching in 1984 in advance of development on the north side of the road going out of the gate showed that the soil was completely free of Roman debris and that the lower levels of grey/black soil were silts, probably deposited by the Lavant, which at one time ran across the land and which undoubtedly flooded many times in the winter and spring. If, as we suspect, the Lavant was diverted around the town walls after the late second-century defences were built,[14] then in addition to cutting off part of the earlier town it must have rendered the land to the north of the road outside the West gate unsuitable for settlement. There is a possibility that a small suburb might exist further out, west of where the Lavant turned south to run into the harbour, but so far no evidence has been forthcoming. The land on the south side, on the site of the present Theological College, was occupied by a cemetery in the fourth century.

Roman Amenities

The public baths

Every Roman town had its public baths, usually built and paid for out of taxation. It was the social centre, where rich and not-so-rich alike would foregather for bathing, exercise and social intercourse. Few, if any, private residences within the town would have their own baths, as bath suites were available to be rented for private parties. Villas outside the town had their own baths, which varied in size and elegance according to the pocket of the owner. Bathing was a symbol of the Roman way of life and both the sauna (dry heat) and turkish (wet heat) methods of bathing were practised.

The basic lay-out was a large *palaestra* or exercise yard where violent exercise was undertaken to promote sweating. After the exercise, the bather proceeded to the disrobing room and thence to the *tepidarium* where the moderate heat would encourage more perspiration. Thereafter, the *caldarium* or hot room was entered where the bather, by now sweating heavily, would be scraped by *strygils* (iron blades) to remove dirt from the skin. A small hot bath in the *caldarium* provided hot water to be poured over the body as well as promoting a good deal of steam in the atmosphere. From the *caldarium* the bather proceeded to the *frigidarium* or cold room, where a plunge in the cold bath would close the pores of the skin and complete the bathing cycle.

The public baths in Chichester are known to lie below the Telephone Exchange in Chapel Street and the Army and Navy Stores in West Street, with the western boundary being below the church of St. Peter-the-Great and the houses to the north of the church on the west side of Tower Street (Pls. 23 & 24). The southern boundary extends south of the Army and Navy Stores and road works in recent years uncovered a large wall in excess of 1.5 metres

34.   Tower Street Excavations, 1974/5. Part of Room 1 of the Roman Public Baths.

wide running east-west below the pavement in front of the store. This must be a stylobate, designed to carry large columns and, on the south side of it, below the street, were traces of pink mortar laid on compacted gravel. We know from elsewhere in West Street (see above p. 31) that the pink mortar was the bedding for large stone flags which have long since been robbed out, but which once formed a flagged open space along the south side of the baths.

The northern part of the baths, which comprised some of the heated suites, was excavated in 1974–5 and the discoveries made then, linked with observation of foundation trenches for the Telephone Exchange in Chapel Street, enabled an estimate of the size of the baths complex of about 5,500 square metres in area. In 1960, when an extension on the north side of Morant's store in West Street (now the Army and Navy Stores) was built, part of a large apsidal wall was found, with a fragment of black and white mosaic nearby (Pl. 29). The apse, which cannot yet be related to other fragments of buildings found since, may have been part of a large cold plunge bath.[15] The mosaic, which is still preserved below the floor of the shop, is discussed on p. 36 above.

It is doubtful whether a complete plan of the baths can ever be recovered, but sufficient was seen during the rescue excavations of 1974–5 to show that there were several periods of alteration, with cold rooms being converted to hot and *vice versa* and with additional stokeholes being built as required. The main fuel for the furnaces was unloaded at the north end of the baths, where there was a hardstanding constructed for the purpose. Judging by the large amounts of ash and charcoal found in the stokeries, faggots were used for much of the time, but charcoal may have replaced faggots towards the middle of the fourth century, as evidence from the Chilgrove villas indicates that it was being used there in the latest period. The water supply was fed to the baths from the north side, from a cistern which still exists below Tower Street, opposite the Public Library. This is discussed in more detail below (*see* water supply). The waste water, of which there was a considerable amount, was flushed out via a subsidiary drain into one of the main sewers which ran east-west along the northern boundary of the baths complex.The baths probably lasted throughout the life of the town, from the later years of Cogidubnus's rule until the early fifth century, and may not have passed from use until the Roman way of life ceased to have any meaning for the inhabitants. There is a possibility that the pumping equipment was still being repaired late on in the fourth century, as carbon 14 and tree-ring dating of the oak timbers recovered from the cistern in 1975 suggest a late fourth-century date for the time that the tree was felled. No evidence for the final abandonment of the baths has so far been found. Heavy robbing of the masonry foundations during the late Saxon and early Norman periods, when supplies of stone were needed, first by Alfred the Great to repair the town walls against the Danes and again in the late eleventh century when the cathedral was being built, would in any case tend to blur the picture.

The water supply

With water so near to the surface, the citizens of Noviomagus dug wells for their supply. Many have been excavated, both inside and outside the town. Some were lined with masonry, usually being constructed of flat sandstone slabs set in stiff yellow clay, with a timber-enclosed box at the bottom. Others were timber-lined throughout. One well, excavated in 1959 outside the walls on the west side of the town where the Avenue de Chartres now runs, belonged to the earlier town and had been cut off when the walls were built at the end of the second century. It had not been cleaned out before it was abandoned and was not much more than 15 feet deep. The timber lining at the bottom was still present, having been preserved from decay by the water, and an interesting number of finds were recovered from the bottom, including part of the wooden bucket, the rope and several complete vessels, among them a glass phial. An oak tree must have grown nearby as thousands of acorns were found in the silt in the bottom.

The water supply to the public baths was pumped up from a stone-lined cistern which had been dug deep into the gravel. The walls were massive – in excess of 2.5 metres wide (Pl. 35), and were designed to support a large masonry tank above. This had been destroyed, but from the debris remaining it could be seen that it had been constructed of masonry and lined with *opus signinum*, a hard pink mortar which was water resistant. A pump raised the water from the cistern into the tank above, creating sufficient head of pressure to supply the baths a few yards away to the south. The water was fed through pipes and, since no trace of ceramic water pipes has been found nor the iron collars which would have joined wooden ones together, it is most likely that lead pipes were used. These would have been much more durable and would have been robbed out for use elsewhere once the baths were finally abandoned. The use of pumps to raise the water created problems, both for the Romans and ourselves. Continuous pumping from the gravel deposits into which the cistern was dug caused 'cavitation' in the gravel as the finer material was removed with the water. As a result, the walls of the cistern started to subside and settle inwards, which made excavation of part of the cistern in 1975 a hazardous undertaking. (Pl. 36) Within the town, the well builders went to considerable trouble to ensure that the water supply was protected against seepage from domestic cess-pits. First, a large square pit was dug into the gravel and lined with timber to keep the gravel from silting back into the hole. Then the stone lining was built above – the masons working from the outside and backfilling the space between the side of the pit and the well lining with gravel and clay, consolidated to prevent the ingress of foul water. There would usually have been a small well-house at the top, and since all Chichester wells are quite shallow, the water would have been easily extracted by bucket and windlass.

The drains

The geology of the coastal plain around Chichester may be summarised as follows: uncultivated topsoil comprises brickearth (clay), with clay-with-flints below. This lies above the coombe deposits (a mixture of gravel and chalk), and below this lies the chalk. The capping of brickearth varies considerably in thickness from less than half a metre above the gravel to over a metre and sometimes more. The gravel below the clay ensures that the water drains away quickly except in the wettest weather, and in early Roman times it was quite easy to dig a well and reach water at a depth of 3–4 metres, depending just where in the town you were. The nearer to the harbour, the nearer to the surface the water is. Intermittent streams (now known as lavants) used to flow when the level of the water in the chalk hills to the north of the town was high enough. The River Lavant still flows today but higher extraction rates by the water authority and the increase in surface water drainage has both lowered the water table

35. Tower Street Excavations, 1974/5, showing part of the cistern supplying water to the Public Baths. The walls, which supported a large masonry tank above, are 2.7 metres thick.

36. Tower Street Excavations, 1974/5. Excavators dismantling the coffer dam sunk into the cistern to recover large timber beams.

and increased the run-off rate, so that now the Lavant only flows for a few months a year, usually during the winter and spring. In Roman times these streams must have flowed nearly all the time except perhaps in very dry summers, when people would have to deepen their wells or dig fresh ones. Surface water drainage was always a problem in wet weather and the town was equipped with sewers to cope with it. Two municipal drains have been located and sectioned in the north-west quadrant, with a possible third one below Marks and Spencer in East Street. Of the other two, one runs east-west below County Hall and may drain into a central sewer below Tower Street, while the other runs to the north of the public baths and drains westwards, collecting the waste water from the public baths and probably discharging into the same central sewer.

Civilisation depends largely upon drains and public hygiene, and it is interesting to study the construction, repair and final decay of the Chichester Roman sewers and see how the fortunes of the town affected the public works department. Several sections were cut across the two sewers in the north-west quadrant and a close study of the one north of the baths showed that it was originally of masonry construction and about 1.7 metres deep. The ditch dug to house the drain was about 3 metres wide at the top but the inside width of the invert was no more than 0.5 metre. The drain would have been boarded in at the top to prevent people and animals falling in, but the covers would be designed to allow access for cleaning out the silt.

We have no firm date for the construction, but as the drains had to take account of the street lay-out it is likely that they were built towards the end of the first century A.D. By that time the public baths were functioning and the drain from the baths to the sewer is one of the earlier features. The evidence for the masonry construction of the Tower Street sewer is well defined, as part of it remained for the excavators to see (Pl. 37), but the situation is less clear about the drain below County Hall, where either it was timber-lined from the start or had been thoroughly robbed of masonry before being reconstructed in wood. We do not know how long the masonry drains lasted, but eventually the one in Tower Street fell into disrepair. As we know from modern experience, public utilities are usually among the first casualties of economic recession and we should look for a period in the history of the province when the times were consistently bad over a long period. The later third century suggests itself. This was a period of great civil unrest; of usurper Emperors who took Britain out of the Empire and a time when business confidence was at a low ebb and the coinage had deteriorated to such a degree that some people buried their money. The revival came in the early fourth century under the Emperor Constantine and an increase in prosperity was reflected in a rebuilding programme within the town and in the surrounding country-side. At about this time the two sewers in the north-west quadrant were re-dug; the collapsed masonry appears to have been robbed out for re-use elsewhere and the drains were lined with planks which had been charred to render them more resistant to decay. The Tower Street drain was not dug so deep on the second occasion and a date for the re-lining with charred timbers is indicated by large fragments of red-coated Oxford-shire wares which were trapped edge-on between the planked lining and the side of the cutting. The pottery has a wide date range, but is not likely to have reached Chichester before the end of the third or the beginning of the fourth century. As time went on, evidence of neglect and decay can again be seen, and finally the timber slot

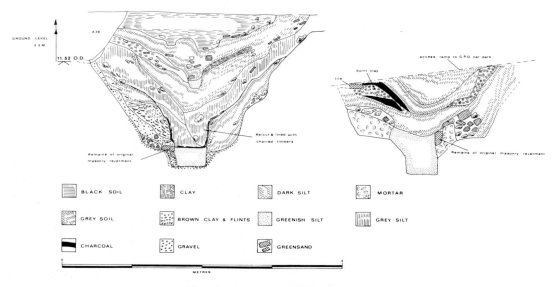

37. Section across a Roman sewer.

at the bottom of the drain silted up and the amount of water that could find a course through it shrank to a sinuous trickle. The timbers rotted away, leaving only the charcoal from the charring process to show where they had been. Later, the timber superstructure must have collapsed, leaving a deep hollow along the line of the original drain which eventually became a tip for rubbish. Parts of it were still being made up, as the ground sank, as late as the medieval period.

Private houses varied in size from large masonry and timber-framed houses like those alongside Chapel Street, to the fairly squalid timber huts of the peasants and artisans. All seem to have dug cess-pits for the disposal of their sewage and, as in medieval times, these would have been dug out from time to time and the manure spread on the fields and gardens. The large house on the north side of the cross roads in Chapel Street (House 2) had a 'service' area opening on to the street where, in the fourth century, the latrines and cess-pits were functioning. The gravelled courtyard of the service area was deep in oyster shells and other debris and was reminiscent of a farmyard. It must have stunk to high heaven in hot weather and have been ankle deep in mud when it was wet. In other towns there is evidence for some of the larger houses having drains that were connected to the main sewers and controlled by outfalls. No such arrangement has yet been seen in Chichester, but that is not to say that it did not exist.

The roads and streets

Everyone who has seen the plan of a Roman town will be familiar with the gridded street plan, with the roads bisecting at right-angles, and a study of many of our ancient towns with Roman ancestry will show that even today the constraints of Roman planning affect 20th-century citizens and traffic. In Chichester, as in Winchester and other *civitas* capitals which later became Saxon *burghs*, the present-day street plan is not Roman, but Saxon, but even the Saxon plan was affected by the Roman as the main streets were forced to leave the town by the original Roman gates from which roads led to the surrounding countryside. This meant that the main streets tended to preserve their original line. The rest of the Saxon streets wander first to one side and then the other of the Roman alignment and this could well be because some of the earliest Saxon houses were actually *on* the old Roman street surface, possibly because it offered a firm foundation relatively free from rubble and vegetation. Excavation at the old Central Girls School in Chapel Street,[16] which straddled a Roman cross-roads, provided examples of this. The whole of the gravelled surface of the streets was pock-marked with the post-holes and pits associated with houses of Saxon settlers. The main streets were probably laid out towards the end of the first century, at some time after the death of Cogidubnus and the establishment of the *civitas*. Undoubtedly, there were streets before this: the military site would have been laid out with streets between the barrack rows and some of these are likely to have continued in use in the later town. All the streets were constructed of gravel, mostly dug from outside the town. The surface was carefully prepared and the gravel laid in thin layers, bonded with clay or sand and each layer rammed down hard. It was cambered to facilitate drainage, usually with a small ditch or channel on both sides. Roman Chapel Street was an exception. It had the remains of a tiled walk-way along the west side and drained from west to east into a small channel which was probably timber-lined and may have had a timber cover. The street gradually became wider with each successive metalling, with the gravel filling the drain and another one being provided further out. The same thing happened in East Street, where the ditch on the south side of the street had almost completely filled with gravel from re-surfacings, but here no second ditch had been provided.

All the Roman streets marked on the plan (Pl. 15) have been proved by excavation. Others can be conjectured, but it is unsafe to assume that the streets are exactly the same distance apart; note the distance between Roman North Street and Chapel and Tower Streets.

The streets were repaired from time to time, not always with freshly dug material. At the Chapel Street cross-roads it was seen that much of the gravel used for making up the roads, especially in the later periods, was old and dirty, with considerable amounts of pottery and other finds mixed in with it. This could only have come from stockpiled material taken from one location and stored for re-use on the roads. As it is highly unlikely that any of the streets were destroyed, it seems that the only source of dirty gravel would have been from old courtyards or other metalled hardstandings. As time went on, the road levels in the more populous parts of the town started to rise. The street surface did not wear evenly and in some instances layers of green silt accumulated in potholes and ruts and these were sealed by the next layer of gravel thrown down and compacted into it.

Much more remains to be discovered of the Roman street plan and it will require many more years of observation before enough of it emerges to allow the rest to be safely conjectured. Sometimes intelligent guesswork combined with fortuitous development along the projected line of a street gives us a little more of the plan, but drawing lines on a map without the back-up of excavation can be a misleading exercise.

As so much gravel was extracted from outside the town it is surprising that signs of the excavations are not visible today. It was noticed that the western lip of the early military ditch in St. Pancras was quarried away, presumably for gravel to surface Stane Street, at some time before the cemetery was established there in about A.D. 70.[17] Other deep pits of some antiquity have been found which are likely to have been dug for gravel, for example, on the site of St. Richard's Hospital when an extension was built in 1968. Here, the pits were still being backfilled in medieval times, and several fine pieces of Roman masonry were found by the contractors. These have now been placed in the District Museum. Reference to the Gardner Map (Pl. 38) shows a number of large ponds which encircle the city from the west side round to the north-east, where the last one is the Dell Hole, now filled in and used as a car park by the Tennis Club. Only one of these ponds is visible today – the large one at the south-west of the town and now south of the College of Technology in what used to be Westgate Fields. Another deep hole which might have been a gravel pit was found during excavation south of the railway line in 1975, and this is on the same line as the others on the Gardner Map.[18] These ponds are impossible to date, but they are almost certainly old gravel workings and some may well date from Roman and medieval times.

The roads outside the town

Four roads radiate from *Noviomagus*. Outside the north gate a road goes to *Calleva Atrebatum* (Silchester), the capital of the northern Atrebates. As it leaves the city it runs roughly on the line of the modern road, diverging from it slightly along the Broyle and going through a gap in the Chichester Dykes. At the top of Heathbarn Down, near Binderton, it changes alignment a few degrees and goes across the top of the down, descending into the valley near Chilgrove 2. From there it goes to Iping where there was probably a posting station in Roman times. The road has not been sectioned near the Chichester end, but the side ditches, 60 feet apart, can be clearly seen, both from the ground and the air, where it passes over Heathbarn Down (Pl. 39).

The road issuing from Eastgate is Stane Street and goes to *Londinium*. The course of this famous road has been traced over most of its route and much has been written about it.[19] Some of it is still a modern highway and in other places the line can be traced where it goes over downland or through woods. A particularly fine stretch is that from Eartham to the top of Bignor Hill, where a terrace-way descends to the villa below. At the Chichester end the road coming out of the gate divides, with St. Pancras (Stane Street) going off in a north-easterly direction whilst the Hornet goes eastwards in the direction of Bognor Regis. While no proof exists, the Hornet may also be a Roman road serving the coastal settlements to the east of the *civitas* capital.

Very little is known of the road to Selsey, which came out of the Southgate and would have linked the flourishing settlements at Selsey, Sidlesham and the Witterings. Gravel metalling on the assumed line was noted outside the Crown Court in Southgate during road works in 1972 and what might have been the side ditches of the road were

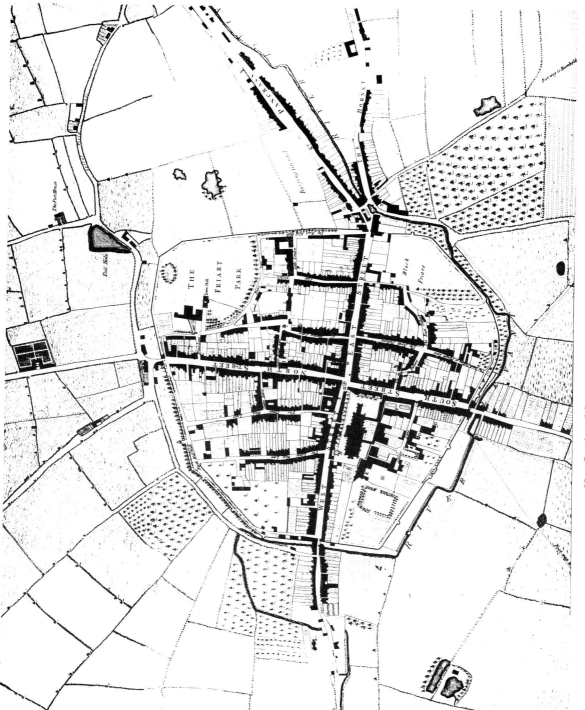

38. Gardner Map showing extra-mural areas.

39.   The Roman road to *Calleva Atrebatum* (Silchester), where it passes over Heathbarn Down to the north of Chichester. The side ditches can be clearly seen, partly overlaid by later field patterns. Looking south.

seen during observations on the gas pipe line laid during 1969 across Kipson's Bank, Hunston.[20] A spread of gravel was noted at this point after ploughing and this might possibly be the remains of the road metalling. The ditches, which were 79 feet apart and aligned north-south, would have marked the limits of Imperial territory.

The road from the Westgate went to *Clausentum* (Bitterne, Southampton) and nothing is known of the eastern end of its course once it leaves the Westgate, although the route is well attested further west. It must have left the gate at an angle, like Stane

Street, and headed north-west.Such an alignment would take it to the north of the palace at Fishbourne which is the only conceivable route, but so far there has been no opportunity to test this hypothesis and the railway line may well have destroyed it at the critical point. It is certain that other roads branched off the major routes to serve settlements and isolated industrial centres and it is popularly supposed that the Birdham Straight is a Roman road which linked up settlements at the Witterings. It could well be so, but a note of caution should be introduced here. Not all straight roads in the Chichester area are of Roman origin. Some are estate roads dating from the eighteenth and nineteenth centuries. Roman roads were not necessarily straight all the time either. They changed alignment to suit the terrain and frequently crossed hills by a series of terraced zig-zags, reverting to their original alignment when the ground permitted. The road surface would vary according to what material was locally available. In and near Chichester the material was gravel, but further north, where the roads crossed the Downs, the surface was rammed flints set in clay or puddled chalk and, in some parts of the Weald, iron slag from nearby iron-workings was used.

The amphitheatre

Most Roman towns of importance had amphitheatres where entertainments were staged for the benefit of the populace. The shows put on in a provincial capital would rarely rise to the expensive heights of gladiatorial combats, but bull and bear baiting, cockfighting, and circus performances, including tumblers and acrobats, would form the usual entertainments, amplified occasionally perhaps by the public execution of criminals.

The amphitheatre at Chichester was outside the town on the south-east side of the town defences, and at the time it was built it was no more than a few yards from the outskirts. Part of the bank surrounding the theatre can still be seen as it is now an open space which can be reached by walking out of the Eastgate along the Hornet and turning right down a narrow passage-way or 'twitten' which forms the north end of Whyke Lane. This might well have been the route in the Roman period as well. Much of the theatre has now been built over, but trial excavations by Miss G.M.White (Mrs Grahame-Clark) in 1935 showed that it was elliptical in plan (Pl. 40) with the long axis about 185 feet and the short axis 150 feet across. The floor of the arena had been excavated to a depth of four feet below Roman ground level and a bank constructed around it which would have held the seating for the spectators. This bank was revetted on the inside by a wall about four feet wide. From the very sparse dating evidence the excavator concluded that it was built between A.D. 70–80 and went out of use by the end of the second century, with the revetting wall being robbed for building stone soon afterwards.[21] Her conclusion should be treated with caution as these were no more than trial excavations and only a small sample of dateable evidence was recovered. It is likely that a date of about A.D. 70 is about right for the construction, but more excavation would be required before a date of late second century can be accepted for its abandonment. While it is true that, on present evidence, the erection of the bank and wall around the city took place towards the end of the second century, it is unlikely that the amphitheatre was abandoned and robbed at the same time unless another had been constructed elsewhere.

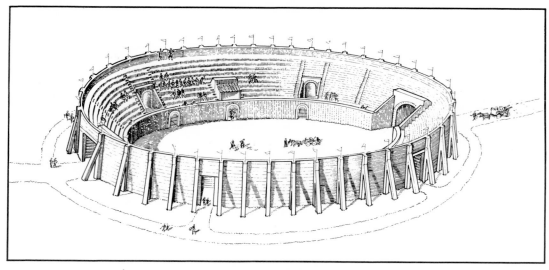

40.   Imaginative reconstruction of the Roman Amphitheatre by Max Wholey.

The defences

The earliest defences were those associated with the legionary occupation of A.D. 43. It was standard military practice to defend encampments by earthworks consisting of a ditch or ditches with a bank and palisade on the inside, and it would have been unthinkable, even in friendly territory, not to have the troops within a defensive perimeter. The early, military-style ditches below the St. Pancras cemetery and the Needlemakers have already been discussed. with the suggestion that they might represent part of an early military 'marching camp' slightly to the east of the later town. At the same time, if the barrack-like buildings below Chapel Street belong to the base camp, then another defensive work may have been constructed around it and this still awaits discovery. Two other earthworks merit discussion. Excavation on the north side of St. Mary's Hospital in 1966[22] revealed an early re-cut ditch associated with pottery of Claudio-Neronian date. Whilst the ditch was not of the proportions to suggest a defensive function it is most likely to have been either a drainage or a boundary ditch, and part of the original military planning. The second ditch was found during excavations at the Theological College in 1985; it was aligned north-south and must have originally have been about 1.4 metres deep. It was of the standard V-shaped profile and had been backfilled with the same material dug from it within a fairly short time. It was associated with a deposit of early imported fine wares from Italy and Gaul – the wares which are invariably found on military sites of the invasion period of A.D. 43.[23] More of this ditch needs to be excavated before its true function can be assessed, but it is just about deep enough to have a defensive function provided additional material was used to construct an adequate bank. But if it *was* defensive, it would have been no more than a temporary affair before either the troops moved away or a more permanent defensive work was established elsewhere. In the event, it was backfilled before any significant erosion of the sides had occurred.

After the military left and the native town developed it has seemed until recently that the town remained undefended until the end of the second century. Now, the discovery of the defensive ditch in the Cattlemarket (above, p. 24) indicates an earlier defensive work which enclosed a different area. The possibilities have already been discussed in Chapter 2, but while no final conclusion can be arrived at until more of the ditch has been traced and a larger sample of pottery examined, we can be fairly sure that it functioned as a defence within the period of Cogidubnus's client kingship. The late second-century defences, of which a considerable part survives today, consisted initially of two V-shaped ditches with an earth bank and a palisade (Pl. 41). Both bank and ditches have been excavated by archaeologists before, the most detailed examination being that undertaken by John Holmes in 1959,[24] when the defences on the south-west corner of the city were sectioned and another section cut through the bank at the rear of the wall along Market Avenue. A study of the soil from the bank indicated that it was constructed from the spoil dug from the ditches and that at some time after the defences had been erected the bank was cut back and a masonry revetting wall built in the front. A similar gap in time between the bank and ditch construction and the building of the

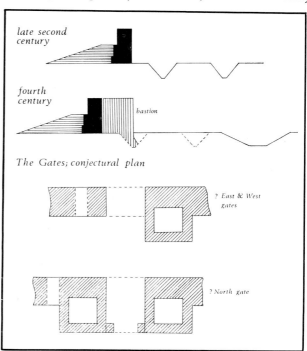

41.   Type diagram of Chichester defences (after A. E. Wilson).

town wall has been noted at Silchester and Winchester, and in all three towns the date suggested for the operation is late second to early third century. It seems to have been part of a comprehensive programme of urban defensive works embarked upon in Britain (alone of the Roman provinces) and affected not only the *civitas* capitals but also many of the smaller towns. Whether this fortification programme was in response to an outside threat, or whether it owed its impetus to Clodius Albinus who succeeded Pertinax as Governor of Britain in A.D. 193 is not clear. Albinus became Caesar under Septimus Severus in 195 and the fortification of the urban centres in Britain may have been in preparation for the forthcoming struggle with Severus for mastery of the Empire.[25] At Chichester, the town defences excluded part of the earlier town, notably outside the North, West and South gates and it might well be that the wall, which enclosed roughly 99 acres, was tailored to fit the forces which might be available to defend it.

The gates

Very little has been discovered of the four main gates. What remained of the superstructure of the late medieval gates was swept away when the town was largely rebuilt in the 18th century, the North, West and South gates being taken down in 1720 and the Eastgate in 1780. No archaeologists were present when this happened, so it is impossible to say whether any Roman work survived in the foundations of the later gateways, but the chances are that some remained. Certainly, it seems that the gates were in their original Roman positions and the woodcut by Grimm (Pl. 42) showing the Eastgate in 1782 may be very similar to the aspect of the Roman gates. Discoveries since the gates were removed have been sparse, but tend to support the view that they were just simple tunnels through the wall; lacking out-thrust drum towers, and with one or perhaps two guardrooms behind.

At Northgate, Dr Wilson noted the remains of walling found below the forecourt of the Northgate Garage when a petrol tank was being installed[26] and he thought it might be the foundations of the east guardroom of the gate. Other service trenches cut through the South gate in 1977 struck part of what might be the east guardroom of that gate, just outside Rumbelows,[27] but more work needs to be done, preferably below the west pavement of Southgate, before we can know whether the gate had two guardrooms or one.

At some time in the fourth century the defences were re-organised, when bastions were added to the walls at intervals. These were designed to carry *ballistae*, which were capable of firing arrows or other projectiles distances of up to 400 yards. The two V-shaped ditches belonging to the earlier defences had by then partially silted up and were filled in. The inner one had weathered back towards the wall and in the places where the bastions were to be built the ditch had to be consolidated with a platform of rammed chalk and flints to take the thrust of the tower, which projected forwards over the inner edge of the ditch. In place of the two ditches another one, wider and flat-bottomed, was dug further away from the wall, providing a 'killing ground' for the defenders. Only seven of the bastions are now known and of these, only five are above ground. Four have been examined by archaeologists and a consideration of the published reports indicates that the construction details of each tower seem to be identical.[28] (Pl. 43)

The provision of the bastions to the defensive circuit implies that there was a detachment of regular troops stationed in the town to operate the *ballistae*. The likeliest date for these additions to the defences would have been shortly after A.D. 367, the year of the great 'barbarian conspiracy' when Britain was overrun by Picts, Scots, Franks and Saxons. Order was restored by Count Theodosius over the next two years following this event and the strengthening of the defences of the Saxon shore followed quickly afterwards. Chichester, being near to the coast, with an accessible harbour that could be used by the *Classis Britannica* would have been a useful sub-station between *Anderida* (Pevensey) to the east and Porchester to the west. The Saxon shore defences had been established in the third century on both sides of the Channel to combat raids on the coasts of Britain and Gaul by Saxons from the Baltic. The raids increased in frequency and severity in the middle and late fourth century.

The only clue to the presence of a late Roman garrison in the town is in the shape of a bronze buckle with zoomorphic decoration (Pl. 44) which is similar to those worn

42. The Eastern or Roman Gate, from a woodcut by Grimm.

43. (*above*) Roman wall and the Bishop's Palace bastion near the south-west corner of the city.

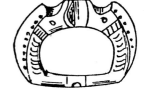

44. (*right*) Late Roman military belt buckle with zoomorphic decoration. Found at County Hall.

by Germanic mercenaries in the late Roman army. It was found in the top of the disused Roman sewer below County Hall. Of the surviving bastions around the walls, the two best examples are those along the south-west quarter, accessible from the Bishop's garden. Here, the wall and bank behind it are well preserved, although only the core of the wall is Roman work. Excavations in Orchard Street in 1981[29] and recent work on the palace bastion in 1984–5 showed that about one metre of the wall had weathered away since the late fourth century when the bastions were added.[30] (Pl. 43). An essential part of the defences would have been an inter-vallum road to enable defenders to be quickly moved from one part of the wall to another. This may still survive in some places, namely North Walls, East Walls and Theatre Lane, and up to the Civil War period it would still have retained some strategic value.

Chapter Four

The People: Life, Death and Religion

Having examined the foundation and growth of Noviomagus from a military camp to a native capital and thence to a regional capital, and having discussed the buildings, marvelled at the sophistication of their organisation and the things they made and wore, we are still faced with a number of unanswered questions. Chief amongst these is, 'What were the people really like?'. We know something of their history and, from a study of their burial customs, we can deduce a little about their beliefs, but we know nothing about the tribal customs of the Atrebates; what their social system was and what system of land tenure was practised and how their way of life was affected by the conquest. 'Who were the nobles?' 'Who was free and who was slave?' are questions which are relevant, but we can only guess at some of the answers and cull what we can from a study of classical writers about happenings in Gaul at the time of Caesar's conquest and just after.

In Gaul, we are told by Caesar,[1] there were three main classes; the *Equites* (the warrior class), the *Plebes* who were little better than slaves, and the *Druids* who were the priestly class wielding great power. It is likely that the basic class structure was the same in Britain as there had been a number of migrations from the Continent over the years; the Parisi in Yorkshire came originally from the Paris area and the British Atrebates themselves had migrated from the Arras region and the tribal customs may have remained little changed. The hierarchy probably consisted of the king or chief at the apex of the pyramid with a class of sub-chiefs or nobles supporting him, each with his dependents, whose origins would have been within the family group. As society developed there would be a class at or near to the bottom of the pyramid who would do all the work, the tilling of the soil and carrying out the many tasks connected with living off the land. Below this class (the *Plebes*) would come the slaves who had been taken in war. This might be a rough approximation to the organisation of tribal society, but we know nothing about land tenure. Was the tribal territory held in common for the whole tribe, so that it could not be disposed of except by the consent of the tribal elders? Was it held within the king's gift, to grant to anyone he chose? How was it divided up and, finally, what were the inheritance laws? The two basic systems of inheritance, 'Primogeniture' (where the eldest son, or daughter in some cases, inherits) or 'Gavelkind' (where the estate is divided among the children), have been known since antiquity, and E.W.Black and others have suggested that 'Gavelkind', or partible inheritance,[2] would account for the large villas, for example Fishbourne Palace and Bignor in the fourth century, extending their living quarters to accommodate up to three or four families who had jointly inherited. This is at present incapable of proof but, if land in the tribe could be inherited, could it be alienated from the tribal lands and sold to an outsider? In Gaul under the Romans it could be, because it could be pledged as security for loans and the land could either be sold or acquired by the debtor as quittance. It is likely that the same applied to Britain after the conquest.

As mentioned in Chapter 3, the *decurions* who served on the *ordo* or council were required to have a property qualification and were drawn originally from the tribal nobles. Other officers, for example the magistrates, had to dig into their pockets for the privilege and by the fourth century, when Roman citizenship had been extended to the provincials, there was little incentive and a lot of expense, which made it an unrewarding task. Society was stratified into the same basic divisions that obtained in Gallic society, but there were opportunities for some people to rise in the world and so there must have been many examples of people working their way up the social ladder in two or three generations. Whilst most people would be more or less tied to the land and to the artisan trades essential in a consumer-orientated society, scope did exist for betterment. The middlemen in society were the *negotiatores* who were often freedmen working for a business house. They would receive into their stores quantities of goods produced or manufactured locally and arrange for the despatch of consignments to other markets. They undoubtedly had a presence in Britain before the conquest and their numbers increased in the wake of the legions who came in A.D. 43, which may help to explain the early and rapid progress of Romanisation in Sussex. They tended to work at recognised markets or *civitas* capitals where there was a legal presence to enforce contracts, and in the immediate post-conquest phase a stable region ruled by a client king friendly to Rome would have been an attractive proposition.

Physical characteristics

We have very little evidence to help us form an opinion of the size and general health of the Romano-British inhabitants of *Noviomagus*. This is mainly because the number of excavated inhumations in Chichester is small (only 92 to date) and most of these were either badly damaged or poorly preserved due to soil conditions. Although one large cemetery at St. Pancras has been partly excavated, all save nine of the burials were cremations, this being the Atrebatic burial rite until about the third century, by which time inhumation was superceding it as the main burial practice. Dr. Helena Barnes studied 14 skeletons from the Eastgate Needlemakers cemetery[3] and concluded that the people buried there were shorter than modern man and most died in their early thirties. Many suffered from osteo-arthritis, but their teeth were generally good, although the grinding surfaces were worn, due probably to abrasive substances in the food. Comparison with Cirencester, where a very large sample from the cemeteries has been excavated and examined by the late Dr. Calvin Wells, gives a fuller picture.[4] Dr Wells reported that the most common complaint affecting the skeletons was osteo-arthritis and he estimated that about 80 per cent of all Cirencester adults suffered from it to a greater or lesser degree. It reflected the daily 'wear and tear' on joints as the result of a physically active and demanding life and is compatible with people living and working on the land and in industries under arduous physical conditions. The commonest areas affected were, as might be expected, shoulders, spine, hip joints, elbows, knees and hands.

The average height of men was 5 ft. 6.5 ins. with a range between 5ft. 3 ins. and 5ft. 10.5 ins. whereas women averaged 5ft. 2 ins. ranging from 4ft. 10 ins. to 5ft. 6.75 ins. This survey was based on 107 males and 44 females. For some reason there were fewer females found in Cirencester, and their average age at death was 37.8 years while the men averaged 40.8 years. There was a very high concentration of lead in the bones and it is thought that this factor could have been the cause of some juvenile deaths.

A preliminary examination by Mary Harman of their Anglo-Saxon successors in the landscape excavated at the sixth-century Saxon cemetery at Appledown, Compton showed that on average a quarter of the people died before the age of 15 and just over a quarter survived beyond 45 years. Three-quarters of the men and half of the women died before that age. Both the men and the women were taller than their Romano-British predecessors, the average height for men being 5 ft. 8.5 ins. (1.7m; sample of 38), and women 5ft. 3.25 ins. (1.62m; sample of 37). This group also had excellent teeth and suffered from osteo-arthritis.[5]

The cemeteries

Under Roman law, no burials were permitted within the city limits and cemeteries were sited outside the gate, usually alongside main roads. Exceptions to this rule were infants who died at birth or shortly afterwards. These were generally given random burial; in gardens, cess-pits, below the eaves of buildings and sometimes beneath hut floors. Several were found buried in the charcoal and ashes raked back in the furnaces in the public baths; possibly the attendants made a sideline of disposing of unwanted babies. Most infants appear to have been buried without much ceremony but occasionally one is found buried in a cist made of roof tiles (see Pl. 45, where a quite elaborate cist was constructed below the eaves of a building in Chapel Street).

Four cemeteries are known outside Chichester (Pl. 15). The most important and, as far as can been seen at present, the earliest, is situated outside the Eastgate on the north side of St. Pancras (Stane Street, Pl. 46).[6] Another is known outside Northgate,[7] where cremations and inhumations were found during roadworks in 1973 (Pl. 47). Two later cemeteries have been found more recently. On the south side of St. Pancras, where the Needlemakers now is, 15 burials belonging to the late Roman period were discovered during excavations in advance of roadworks and building in 1976 and 1978[8] (Pl. 48). Only the northern part of this cemetery, which consisted entirely of inhumations, was established and more burials must lie below the gardens of houses fronting on to the south side of St. Pancras. Finally, between 1985 and 1987 some 59 inhumations were found outside Westgate during building development in the grounds of the Theological College (Pl. 49). These appear to be of fourth-century date.[10] So far, no cemetery is known outside the Southgate, but when the Canal basin was dug in 1819, workmen found a skeleton and a large number of silver coins in a pot, and this may be an indication that there is a cemetery in the vicinity. A further pointer exists in the form of two tombstones, now in the Guildhall Museum in Priory Park, which were found in a pit near the Southgate (see below, p. 65 and Pl. 53), However, trial excavations on a number of likely sites outside the Southgate in recent years have so far failed to locate it.

Out of the large sample of 326 burials from the St. Pancras cemetery,[11,12] only six had coins deposited with them. The practice of placing a coin with the burial derives from Greek and Roman classical tradition, and was the fee required by the ferryman (Charon) to take the soul of the dead person across the River Styx. The tiny proportion of coins in the cemetery is a good indication that it was mainly a native one and that the tradition of the ferryman and his fee was not believed in at that time, although by the fourth century the custom had become widespread in Britain. Only nine of the St. Pancras burials were inhumed, which is another indication of an early date for the

45.   Infant burial in tiled cyst.

46.   Plan of St Pancras cemetery.

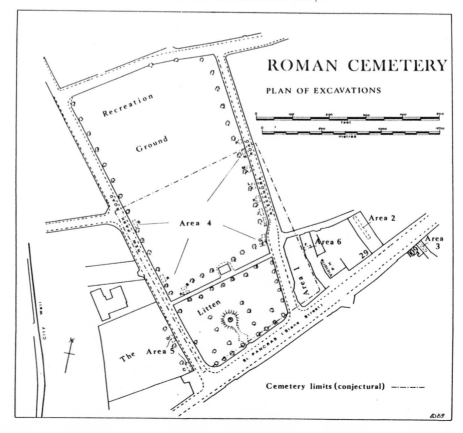

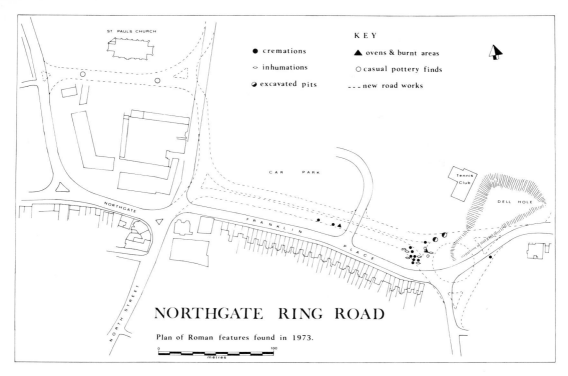

KEY

● cremations ▲ ovens & burnt areas
○ inhumations ○ casual pottery finds
◕ excavated pits --- new road works

NORTHGATE RING ROAD

Plan of Roman features found in 1973.

0 _____ 100
metres

47.   Plan of Northgate cemetery.

48.   Plan of Eastgate Needlemakers cemetery.

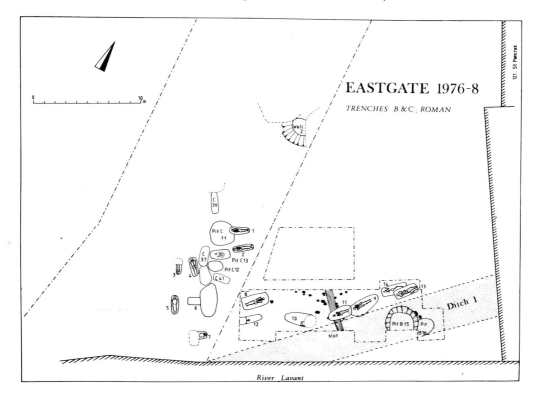

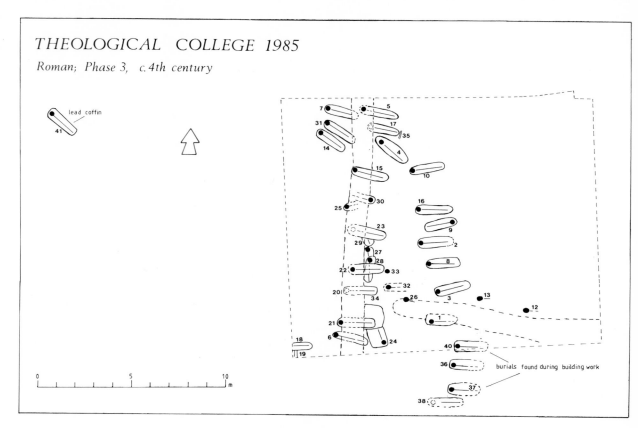

THEOLOGICAL COLLEGE 1985

Roman; Phase 3, c.4th century

49.   Plan showing fourth-century burials at the Theological College, Westgate.

cemetery. They were all later insertions, and some had disturbed earlier cremations. Two of the bodies had been buried with the knees flexed and the remainder were supine and randomly orientated. One late fourth-century burial near the north-west limits of the cemetery had bronze bangles on the arms and ankles, a bronze ring on the left hand and the remains of a late Roman gilded 'crossbow' brooch near the throat. The brooch is the latest dated artifact from the cemetery.

All the grave goods deposited with the cremations had one common characteristic; they were damaged or incomplete in some way. For example, brooches were either damaged or lacked a pin. Bone hairpins and bronze needles were broken before being placed in the grave and the pottery vessels were either chipped or broken in antiquity or were kiln wasters or obvious 'seconds'. The pattern is too regular to be coincidental and it seems that only articles which were ritually 'killed', or were unsuitable for use by the living, were acceptable as grave goods. Some burials were contained within cists made of roof tiles and it seems certain from the pattern of nails discovered with some of the larger burials that they were placed in wooden boxes, probably with a removable lid to allow the pouring of libations. Poorer burials were usually left with the mouth of the flagon protruding from the ground for the same purpose. There is evidence for ritual meals in the numbers of mutton bones, oysters, mussels and chicken left in platters in some graves. Knife cuts on some bones may perhaps indicate that the mourners might have eaten part of the meal at the graveside (Pl. 50 & 51).

At Northgate, a considerable part of the cemetery must lie beneath the car park and tennis courts and may well extend northwards below Oaklands Park. It appears to be later than the one at St. Pancras as the burials were placed there after the defences were established and some were cut through pits belonging to the earlier town, parts of which were left outside the walls when they were built. Of the 17 burials found during the construction of the new road, six were inhumations and, although the sample is small, the high proportion of inhumations suggests a later date. One cremation had a very fine brooch inlaid with millefiori enamel deposited with the bones and half a silver ring into which a silver *denarius* of Caracella had been set as a bezel (Pl. 59.6). The coin dates to A.D.200, which means that the burial cannot have been placed there until the early third century at the earliest.

The few burials from the Needlemakers site outside Eastgate were all inhumations and showed some interesting characteristics. It is unfortunate that the grubbing out of several large trees on the banks of the Lavant and continuous occupation of the site since medieval times has destroyed a number of others. Two of the bodies appear to have been buried in quicklime, and one skeleton was minus all the cervical vertebrae and might have been decapitated. It was buried in a large coffin with very large spikes securing the corners, and the skull was further away from the body than would have been normal. In two other graves, only the skull was present, one with two small New Forest beakers beside it.

Decapitation was used in the fourth century as a means of executing criminals, but it is also known as a burial rite, although usually the head was placed in the grave, either between the knees or at the feet. There is some evidence that some of the graves were not being marked. One body had a fourth-century coin in the skull and the partially articulated leg from another burial deposited in the grave when it was back-filled, which must mean that the earlier body had not decomposed before the later grave was dug through it (see Pl. 52). Apart from the coin in the skull, which was worn and cannot be dated closely, and the two New Forest pots, which have a date range of early fourth to early fifth century, there were no grave goods at all with any of the burials. One of the graves had disturbed a hoard of third- and fourth-century coins, but these had been buried in a pot before the land became a graveyard. Several empty graves were found, each with a layer of silt in the bottom, indicating that they had remained open for some time after being dug.

We do not yet know the extent of the Needlemakers cemetery. It extends northwards from the north bank of the Lavant for a few yards (Pl. 48), but since the River Lavant in its present course might well post-date the Roman period there is a possibility that the cemetery extends as far south as the north side of the Hornet. It is likely that the cemetery was established in the late fourth century and went on into the fifth. The disturbed coin hoard could not have been deposited much before c. mid-fourth century and possibly later still. The only coin to be found with a burial was a very worn and illegible fourth-century type which probably circulated for many years before being placed in the grave. The small suburb along the south side of St. Pancras appears to

50. Two burials from St Pancras, showing the earlier cremation with a pair of sandals or boots deposited in the grave, partly overlaid by a later, crouched inhumation.

51. Cremation burial from St Pancras Roman cemetery.

52. Late or sub-Roman burials from Eastgate Needlemakers.

have been abandoned in the late fourth century and one of the wells serving the houses (Well 2) was robbed of stonework and back-filled with a great deal of surface rubbish including late colour-coated fine wares from the Oxford and New Forest kilns which were still producing after A.D. 350. The coins from the well included several of Valens or Valentinian with a terminal date of A.D. 378. Bearing these points in mind it seems likely that a date of between c. 390 and 420 could be proposed for the abandonment and backfilling of the well, with the extension of the cemetery northwards across the abandoned settlement coming later still.

Until a much larger sample of burials in this cemetery can be excavated it would be unwise to speculate too far either about the burial customs or the extent. All that can be said at present is that the burials excavated indicate a late or perhaps sub-Roman graveyard and that the people buried there were poor. Such a graveyard might fit well into the picture of the declining quality of life, where plague and poverty were facts that had to be coped with, alongside the need to maintain a defence against Saxon raiders at the same time as cultivating the soil on a subsistence basis.

The cemetery outside the Westgate was discovered in 1985 during trial excavations on the site of the Theological College (Pl. 49). It was known from previous work in 1959[13] that part of the earlier town on the west side had been left outside the defences when these were constructed and the 1985 excavations located the remains of the houses and found that a cemetery had later developed on the site, probably at some time in the late third century. Fifty-nine inhumations have so far been discovered, two buried in lead coffins, but the limits of the graveyard could not be established as the excavators were restricted to the areas to be built upon. It is likely that it was quite small, with the northern boundary being on the south side of the Roman road issuing from Westgate, which is unlikely to follow the modern alignment. The eastern limits are just west of the fourth-century defensive ditch which runs below the Avenue de Chartres, and the southern boundary may well be the point at which the burials petered out. To the west, the boundary may extend below the graveyard of St. Bartholomew's church (previously the Church of St. Sepulchre), which was destroyed during the siege of Chichester in 1642. Very few tombstones survive from the town. This is because suitable building stone is hard to come by and the robbing of Roman masonry buildings in Roman and post-Roman times for every scrap of building material has denuded the cemeteries as well. The only two surviving inscriptions on gravestones were found 'at a depth of 7 feet near Southgate'[14] and had been broken and probably re-used in Roman times. One bears the inscription in three lines:

CCA AELIA
CAVVA
AN XXXVI

This was interpreted by Professor Haverfield as BODICCA AELIA CAVVA FILIA ANNOREM XXXVII, which can be translated as either 'Boudicca Aelia Cauva daughter of .:... aged 37, or 'Boudicca Aelia of the Cauvan tribe. . .' A second inscription (Pl. 53) reads:

CATIA
CENSORIN (A)
AN XXIII

Both tombstones were dated to the end of the first century A.D. from the style of the

53. Tombstone found near Southgate, inscribed CATIA CENSORIN(A) AN XXIII.

lettering. A third tombstone was found when Friary Close was being built, but it has since been lost. It was drawn by Thomas King at the time, and reads:

M

NVSAT

IRIVS

LXXXV

This was expanded by Professor Haverfield to read:

DIS MANUBIS ......NVS ATRIARIVS ANNOREM LXXXV

'To the gods of the Underworld ...nus the porter, aged 85 years.'

Religious beliefs

The chief deities of the Roman Empire were Jupiter, Juno and Minerva and the Romans also encouraged the Imperial cult involving the worship of dead Emperors (Divi) and the veneration of the *numen* of living ones. The gods of other tribes and nations within the Empire could generally be equated with those in the Roman Pantheon, and there was a remarkable tolerance towards religious beliefs with the exception of Christianity, which for a long time was held to be a secret and subversive society rather than a religion.

In Chichester there are two inscriptions which relate to the Domus Divina; one, the temple of Neptune and Minerva, was dedicated on the authority of King Cogidubnus and dates to the first century (Pl. 18) and the other is the inscription dedicated to Jupiter Optimus Maximus (Pl. 26),[15] which is roughly contemporary. These two inscriptions indicate that, in Chichester at least, the official Roman state religion was given full expression.

Little is known of Celtic gods and nothing of local ones. All we can be sure of is that the small temples and shrines dotted around the countryside would have a local deity who could generally be identified with a classical god and to whom anyone could make an offering. Within the town, the temples of the 'official' cults would serve as a focus of loyalty for the citizens.

One altar is known from Chichester, found in North Street in 1823 on the site of the Little Anchor Inn (now No. 85).[16] This read:

GENIO S(ACRUM) LUCULLUS AMMINI FIL(IUS) D(E) S(UO) P(OSUIT)
'Sacred to the Genius, Lucullus son of Amminius at his own charge placed this stone'.

This, as it implies, is a dedication to the genius or spirit of the place. It has been suggested[17] that the Lucullus referred to may have been the son of the Amminius (or Adminius) who was a son of Cunobelin and who is thought to have ruled in Kent for a short while in the 30s before being expelled by his father. This dissident son of Cunobelin may have found a welcome in Atrebatic territory after his expulsion from Kent and might even have ruled under Verica and have been allowed to issue silver coins. Four silver minims are known which have the letter 'A' set within interlaced arcs which form a star-like pattern, and two of these were found in the Chapel Street excavations. It is likely, in view of the power struggle going on between the Atrebates and Catuvellauni, that a dispossessed son of Cunobelin would be welcomed by Verica and it is possible that he might have allowed Amminius to mint coins and that the four (Pl. 2.3), all found in or near to West Sussex, may refer to him. Amminius left Britain with a few followers about A.D. 40 and surrendered to the Emperor Caligula at Mainz, but whether he headed an embassy sent by Verica, or was acting on his own behalf is not known. Caligula, who was under the impression that the whole of Britain was being surrendered to Rome, wrote to the Senate and prepared an invasion force, which in the event did not sail as the troops mutinied. It was not until three years later that the invasion finally left Gaul, this time in response to an appeal by Verica in person.

The altar, if it was in its original position when found, would have been near to the centre of the town, and Henig and Nash[18] suggest that it could only have been placed there by an important or distinguished person of whom the authorities approved. The son of a Catuvellaunian prince who had been befriended by Verica might well fit into that category. Dr Henig dates the inscription (now much eroded) as 'early', either Flavian or possibly Neronian, which would fit well with the Jupiter and Cogidubnus inscriptions.

Temples

Only one temple is known within the town, although it must be certain that others existed. The temple of Neptune and Minerva is attested by the Cogidubnus inscription, found in 1723 when a cellar was being dug at the corner of Lion Street and North Street. The inscription may not have been far from its original position when it was found, and street works in 1977[19] showed that there was a substantial tile-bonded wall aligned north-south on the east side of North Street (Pl. 15), only a few yards from where the tablet was discovered. The wall was joined at right angles by one from the east, and it is likely that these foundations belong to the temple. Slightly south of this point and in front of the Council House was the remains of another substantial wall apparently belonging to a different building, which runs eastwards below the Council House and 73 North Street. The wall had an offset in it, and it is just possible that it might be part of the west side of a temple similar to the one excavated at Lydney, Gloucestershire, by Sir Mortimer Wheeler (Pl. 54B),[20] although the latter is a rural pilgrimage site and not strictly comparable.

Other temples are known outside the town. There is one on the top of Bow Hill, excavated many years ago by Carlyon Britton. The results were never published and the papers have unfortunately been lost; all that remains of the evidence is a list of coins, of which the latest was Theodosian (A.D. 379–395) and a verbal account given to the author by Lt. Col. Shaw who dug with Carlyon Britton as a schoolboy. The site, which overlooks the Roman villas in the Chilgrove valley, is an impressive one, and must have served as the shrine for many of the farms in the valleys on both sides of Bow Hill. The coin series goes on later than those from the Chilgrove villas, possibly because at the latest time that the temple was functioning the villas had abandoned a money economy for most practical purposes. There is another temple near Ratham Mill at Bosham, known only as a crop-mark seen from the air and by a scatter of pottery in the ploughsoil (Pl. 54A), but the most important one to be excavated in the area under modern conditions is at Hayling Island. This site, which luckily survived the attentions of the late Dr. Talfourd Ely in the years 1897–1907, was not proved to be a temple until the present series of excavations commenced in 1976.[21] They are now complete and the report is in progress at the time of writing, but it has been established that the first temple was erected in the late Iron Age and consisted basically of a circular shrine within a square enclosure (Pl. 55). The temple was clearly an important one at this time and the excavators found an impressive number of votive objects within the precincts. Some of these were of military equipment, giving rise to the speculation that the temple may have been dedicated to a Celtic war god. The excavators consider it possible that the building of the temple coincided with the arrival in Britain from Gaul of the Belgic leader Commius (see above, p. 1).

Soon after the invasion of A.D. 43 and probably at some time in the reign of Nero, the temple was re-built in masonry on a larger ground plan and the excavators see this as part of the programme of Romanisation undertaken by King Cogidubnus during the early years of his client kingship, probably at the same time that he was building the proto-palace at Fishbourne and developing his native capital at Chichester. The new temple comprised a *cella* or central shrine, circular like its Iron Age predecessor, and about 45 feet in diameter. It was surrounded by a square *temenos* or courtyard and enclosed by a double wall. It appears to have ceased functioning by the early third century.

Reference has already been made to the inscription from Eastgate Needlemakers (see above, p. 22), where the unknown *arkarius* or Treasurer dedicated a shrine to the

54. Roman temples: (A) Ratham Mill, Funtington (conjectural plan from an aerial photograph by J. R. Boyden). (B) Lydney, Glos. (after Wheeler). (C) Conjectural plan of the Roman building at Bosham, possibly a temple (after E. W. Black).

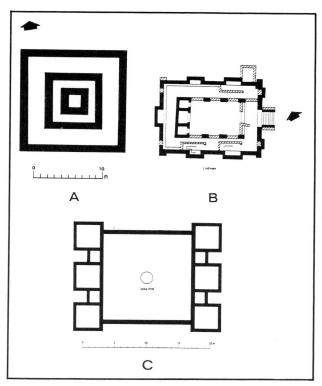

A

B

C

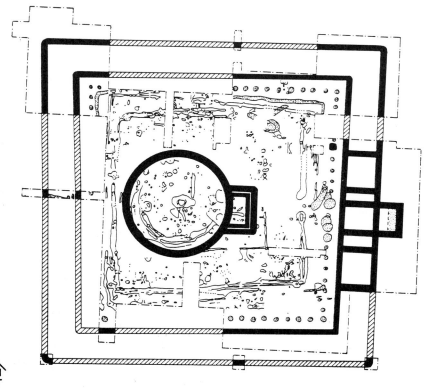

⌇ Iron Age features

▬ Roman walls – known

⫽ Roman walls – conjectured

⊙ Other Roman features

0 5 10 15 20m

55. The Roman temple at Hayling Island.

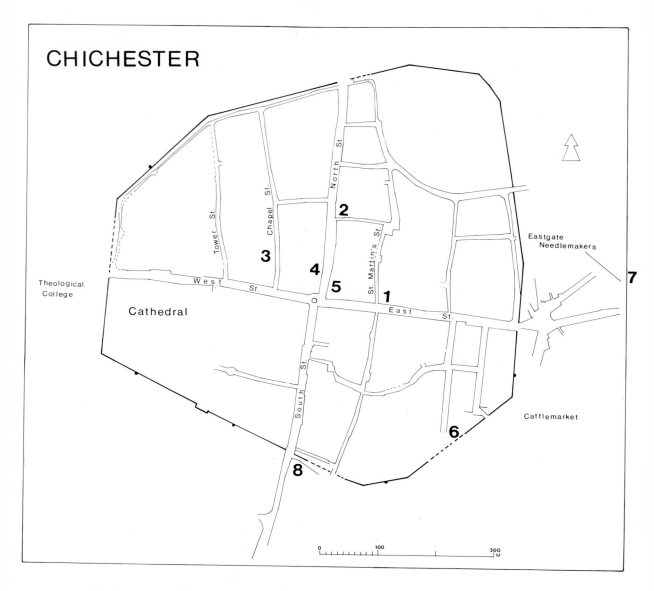

56.　Map showing find-spots of Roman inscriptions and a possible statue base. (1) Nero inscription found at the corner of East Street and St Martin's Street in 1740, and lost soon afterwards. (2) The Cogidubnus inscription found in 1723 below a shop at the north corner of Lion Street and North Street, now mounted on the west wall of the Council House in North Street near to the find-spot. The inscription may have been in its original position in the Temple of Neptune and Minerva, when found. (3) Column base or statue dedicated to Jupiter Optimus Maximus; now in the Guildhall Museum in Priory Park. (4) Site of the base of an altar or statue, noted during redevelopment of Nos. 3, 4 & 5 North Street. (5) Altar, found in 1823 on the site of the *Little Anchor Inn*, North Street (now demolished). Dedicated by Lucullus, son of Amminius. Now in the Guildhall Museum, Priory Park, much eroded after earlier neglect, only one letter surviving. (6) part of a tombstone found in 1809, built into the south-east city wall and later into a wall in the Bishop's Palace; present location unknown. (7) Part of an inscription dedicated to the *Matres Domesticae*. Now in the District Museum in Little London. (8) Two tombstones found near Southgate in 1833. Now in Guildhall Museum, Priory Park.

Matres Domesticae, or 'Mothers of the Homeland'. The main centre of the cult was in Germany, at Bonn, where they were associated with the *Matronae Aufaniae.* The Aufaniae were shown in carved relief with large hats or head-dress and seated in niches surmounted by pediments. The Chichester inscription probably came from a large shrine in which were placed seated statues of the *Matres Domesticae.* It may have been within the town, but equally likely could be near the findspot – outside the Eastgate and near the road to *Londinium.* Perhaps future work near the Needlemakers may locate it.[23] (Pl. 56).

Finally, it has recently been suggested that the Roman buildings discovered in 1832 at Broadbridge Farm, Bosham, might be interpreted as a temple, *possibly* with an associated theatre (*Mitchell* 1866; *Black* 1985).[24] Apart from a small rescue excavation near the site in 1967 by Mrs Rule (*Pitts* 1979),[25] no modern archaeological investigation has been made of this site but, in view of the important implications the discovery of a temple complex near to the *civitas* capital would have for Roman archaeology in this region, several seasons of research excavation by the District Archaeological Unit would seem to be a high priority. (Pl. 54C)

Chapter Five

Trade and Industry

During the later Iron Age, the development of nucleated settlements along the coastal plain and in the valleys to the north indicates that arable farming and stock raising were becoming more intensive. In the second and first centuries B.C. there was trade between the southern coastal regions of Britain and Gaul, with goods, especially wine and oil, finding their way from the Mediterranean by land and water up to the Armorican (Brittany) coast and thence across to Hengistbury Head in Dorset.[1] By the mid-first century B.C. after the conquest of Gaul by Caesar, ships from the Seine estuary were landing cargoes in the harbours around the Solent, including Dell Quay and Fishbourne, and had penetrated up the Thames as far as Hertfordshire. Amongst the goods brought into Chichester Harbour was a wine amphora stamped AVALER, which ended up beneath the old Central Girls School in Chapel Street, and it dates somewhere between 10 B.C and A.D. 10 at the latest. Other amphorae classified as Dressel 1B dating to the same time have been found at the Cattlemarket site[2] and, more recently, the handle of an even earlier amphora (Dressel 1/Pasqual 1) has been identified at the Theological Collége.[3] These finds are a clear indication of pre-Conquest trade with the Chichester region and must point to an Iron Age settlement not far from the present town.

Once Gaul was under Roman rule the cross-Channel trade increased considerably and consisted mainly of wine, fine table-ware of pottery and glass and various kinds of attractive jewellery; in return (according to Strabo iv, 1, 14) the British exported grain, cattle, iron, hides, slaves, gold, silver and hunting dogs. No gold or silver could be mined in the Chichester region, but the other items on the list could be supplied from local resources and were available for export.

After the imposition of the *pax Romana* in the south of Britain from A.D. 43 bringing an end to inter-tribal conflict, the region seems to have rapidly developed into a major food producing area. In the early days, the impetus to produce a surplus above what was needed for domestic consumption was provided by the need to pay taxes and by the development of the *civitas* capital, where there was a market for the corn, beef, pork, mutton, wool, hides and leather goods produced by the farms. The coastal region also produced fish and shell-fish (oysters, mussels and winkles), the first two in large quantities and the third in small, to judge by the numbers of shells found on Roman sites within the city and in the villas. It would also provide salt, a most important commodity, which in Iron Age and earlier times was produced in small amounts along the saltings around the harbours, using crudely baked clay receptacles (briquetage) as containers for transporting it. As the salt was obtained by evaporation of the sea-water, it follows that the industry was seasonal, occupying only the summer months, and the use of briquetage seems to end shortly after A.D. 43. This may mean no more than the adoption of better production techniques, using metal vats on a larger scale, which is quite feasible, as the vats, being valuable, would be removed when production ceased, whereas vessels of baked clay were frequently broken and left on site. Before a full money economy developed under the Romans, salt would have been valuable, not only as a preservative and for flavouring, but also, in its briquetage containers, as a form of currency. After the conquest the latter function ceased, but with an increase in food production implied by the need to provide for urban communities and pay taxes to the government, there is likely to have been a higher demand for the product.

Agriculture, salt production and fishing appear to have been the major primary products of the Chichester region, as they were for many centuries afterwards. Other industrial activity common to Romano-British communities in the area are discussed in detail below.

Urban industry

Shortly after the Second Legion left Chichester, probably between A.D. 45–46, part of the area where the barracks had been located became the site of a pottery industry. Two kilns were found in Chapel Street, below the playground of the Girls' School (Pl. 16), which were making a wide range of vessels, from pear-shaped, bead rimmed vessels in the Atrebatic tradition to carinated bowls and 'two-tone' rusticated beakers and flagons of a similar fine quality and appearance to those being manufactured in Gaul and supplied to the legions.[4] The degree of sophistication and elegance of some of the wares indicates the presence of highly skilled craftsmen, and it is tempting to conclude that they may have been ex-legionary potters who stayed after the legion had left, to produce wares for a new native market. The quality of the products indicates that they were intended to compete with the flood of fine wares beginning to come in from Gaul and Italy. The kilns date from the early years of Nero's reign and the pottery has been found on sites inside and outside the town, e.g. Fishbourne, Halnaker, Cattlemarket and Greyfriars. No other pottery kilns have been found in or near to the city, but the site of a kiln or kilns is known at Rowlands Castle, just over the Hampshire border. The kilns were producing the ubiquitous grey and black wares, but they have not been extensively excavated and a comprehensive pottery report is not yet available so that the date range and pottery styles cannot be assessed. However, it seems certain that other kilns must have sprung up in the early years of the Roman occupation and some of these might well have been just inside or outside the town, where the native potters would have been quick to exploit the increased market. The local London and Reading Beds clays are highly suitable for potting and, with an abundance of fuel handy, locally based enterprises could expect to do well initially. There must have been a kiln near to the city in the late first and early second centuries which was making lead-glazed pottery, possibly in an attempt to compete with the import of red-glossed samian wares from Gaul. Seven of these glazed vessels were found during the excavation of the St. Pancras Roman cemetery, and one was found to be a badly fired waster which could not have travelled far from the manufacturing centre. As time went on and communications improved, the pottery making and distribution became concentrated in specialist hands, and industries of considerable importance grew up in areas best suited for their development. In the early days of the province most of the fine table wares were imported from Gaul, Italy and the Rhineland. Later on, with the growth of regional production centres like those in Dorset, the New Forest, Oxford, Alice Holt near Farnham, the Nene valley and Colchester, most of the British-produced fine wares found their way to the city either by road or water. This system worked

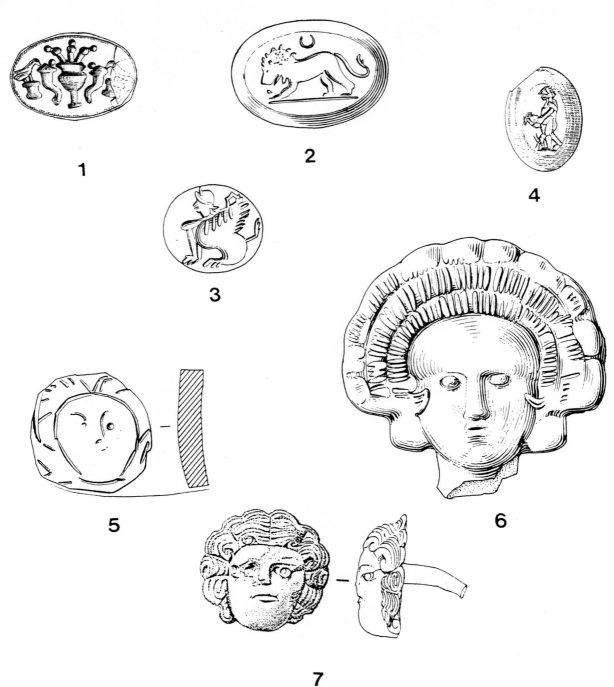

57. Scale 3 times actual size unless otherwise stated. (1) Intaglio of clear glass. The device is a small vessel with three plants in it with a cornucopia on each side, and two birds feeding. From the Cattlemarket. 1st century A.D. (2) Glass paste intaglio portraying a lion with a crescent moon above. From Tower Street site. First century A.D. (3) A sard intaglio portraying a Sphinx with recurved wings, wearing a wreath around the head. Dated to the earlier part of the first century and may be from a ring worn by a legionary. From the Wool Store site, Chapel Street. (4) Intaglio carved from nicolo and portraying Apollo playing a lyre. Late 1st/early 2nd century A.D. From the Cattlemarket. (5) Carved bone 'trial' piece, probably intended to represent Medusa. From Chapel Street. Scale approx. $1^1/_2$. (6) Pipeclay figurine made in central Gaul. The hairstyle suggests a date of manufacture between A.D. 80 and 120. Probably from a 'portrait' bust of a female member of the Imperial Court. These figurines were mass-produced for purchase by the lower classes of provincial society. Scale approx. $1^1/_2$. From the Chapel Street site. (7) Medusa-head on a cast bronze stud, probably from a casket. From the Cattlemarket. Scale approx. $1^1/_2$.

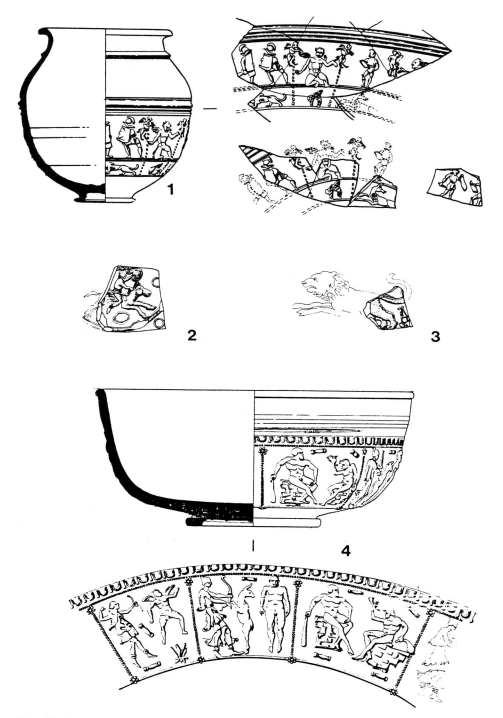

58.   (1) Decorated Lezoux ware, *c.*A.D. 120–135. (2) Samian ware; mounted warrior; Lezoux, A.D. 140–165. (3) Samian ware; Lion, Lezoux, A.D. 145–170. (4) Samian ware, Lezoux, A.D. 120–140. The figures are (*left to right*) Diana, Putto, Diana and stag, nude man, Hercules, Satyr.

well until the late fourth century, when the money supply dwindled and dried up, but this is discussed in more detail in the final chapter.

An assessment of the refuse found in Roman cess-pits (always the richest source of information) shows that a range of luxury goods was coming into the town from shortly after the conquest, mainly imported from Italy and Gaul. As well as the fine pottery mentioned above, elegant glass vessels and pottery lamps are found in the discarded rubbish from the better class houses and also deposited in the cremation cemeteries. Pipe-clay figurines of gods and deified members of the Imperial house are occasionally found, mass-produced in Germany for the less well-off who could not afford alabaster or marble statuettes (Pl. 57–62) Imports of wine from Italy in the pre-conquest Iron Age have already been mentioned. By the end of the first century A.D., galleys were bringing amphorae, made and filled in southern Spain, into the harbours along the south coast. Not all the amphorae contained wine; in fact most had olive oil or fish products in them while others carried *defrutum*, a sweet liquid obtained by boiling down the *must*. Amphorae must have been the first of the non-returnable containers with which we in the 20th century are so familiar. After the contents had been decanted and used, they could be re-used as water containers, storage jars, burial urns, urinals and finally, when broken, were very useful for paving footpaths and courtyards.

There was always a good market for roofing tiles, especially for buildings which were mainly of timber construction, where a non-flammable roof covering would reduce the risk of fire. The products were: baked clay *tegulae* (flanged roof tiles), *imbrices* (ridge tiles), box flue tiles and *pilae* tiles for use in hypocausts. The large flat base and capping tiles used in the under-floor heating arrangements were also useful as quoins in flint walls. A tile kiln is known at Dell Quay, where there are suitable supplies of Reading Beds clay, and others have been found at Hartfield[5] and Itchingfield.[6] Still more may await discovery.

Stone roof tiles were also used for houses in Chichester and at Chilgrove. These were mainly kite-shaped sandstone tiles from the Horsham region, although some from

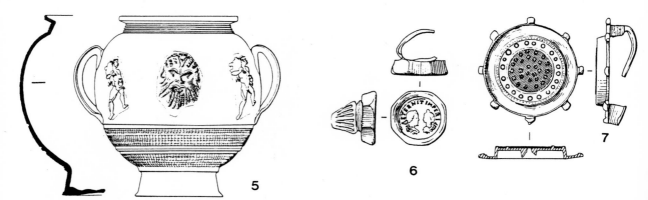

59.   (5) Black Samian goblet with masks of Pan and Satyr, Lezoux, A.D. 120–145. Two objects from cremation (Burial No. 3), Northgate Roman Cemetery. (6) Silver ring with a *denarius* of Caracalla and Severus as the bezel. The coin dates to *c.*A.D. 200. (7) Bronze disc brooch with millefiori decoration.

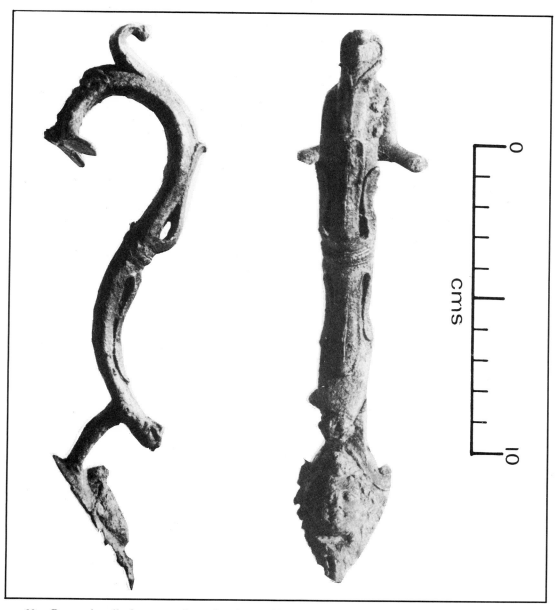

60.   Bronze handle from an *askos* or jug from which wine was poured. This is a finely-cast piece with applied silver foil highlighting the elaborate decoration. The escutcheon carries the head of a young satyr. The extremely fine workmanship suggests an Italian origin and, as far as present knowledge goes, this is the only *askos* handle recorded in Britain. Found during excavations east of the Roman Palace at Fishbourne in 1986.

61.   Impression from an intaglio found in Chapel Street, Chichester, in 1977 during excavations. Cut in green chalcedony, it portrays a satyr seated in front of two flutes, leaning against a rock. One of the finest gemstones found in Britain, it dates to the early first century A.D. (scale: 3.5/1).

the Bembridge quarries on the Isle of Wight found their way to Chapel Street in the fourth century and were used on House 2. The kite-shaped tiles were secured to the roof by a single nail, but the presence in the collapsed building rubble at Chilgrove 1 of imbrices and tegulae indicates that the ridge and the bottom edge of the roof were finished off with the standard baked clay tiles.[7]

Metal working

At about the same time that the pottery kilns were established in the Chapel Street area, part of the same site housed a bronze-working industry. Many hundreds of small crucibles were found, some in association with small hearths. Analysis of the vitreous glaze found on the rims showed that lead was present, and this is an indication of enamelling. The small size of the crucibles shows that the craftsmen were enamelling jewellery and it is likely that this was also being made on the site.

Their products could well have included some of the fine brooches, bangles, rings and hairpins that are frequently found on Chichester sites.

The one essential industry was iron. It was the key metal, without which organised Roman life would have been impossible to sustain. The tools, weapons and fittings used in everyday life (think how many nails, each one hand-forged, were needed to construct even a small house) were all made of iron and the Regni were particularly fortunate to have a major source of iron ore within the kingdom. There is no doubt that the exploitation of Wealden iron, begun in the Iron Age, reached very high levels during the Roman period. It would have been smelted and worked up into 'blooms' on site and then shipped, either by water or road, to the towns and settlements to be forged by blacksmiths. We know from excavations in the Cattlemarket[8] that there was a considerable amount of iron forging carried out in the fourth century; both of the Chilgrove villas had iron forging hearths in the latest phase, and the existence of large quantities of forging slag outside the east, south and west gates of the city indicates the presence of smithies nearby – placed outside the town as a precaution against fire. The 13th-century city fathers followed the same practice and ensured that the pottery kilns were outside the town on the south and west sides. (Pls. 63 & 64)

Other Crafts

Amongst the crafts practised by local people were manufacturing of bone tools and trinkets and leatherworking. Large numbers of bone hairpins, some beautifully carved, are found on Chichester sites, and other items include needles, dice-boxes, combs,

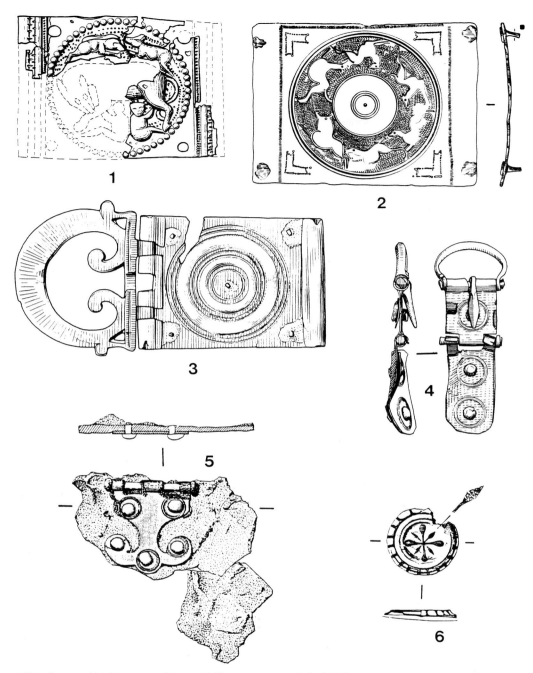

62. Items of legionary equipment (all approx. actual size). (1) Embossed bronze belt-plate from the *cingulum* (the legionary's belt), bearing the wolf and twins motif. (2) A very fine brass belt plate with a hunting scene, showing five dogs chasing a boar. (3) Legionary belt buckle with a hinged belt plate attached. (4) Bronze buckle and strap from the segmentated cuirass (*lorica segmentata*). (5) Iron plate with half of a bronze lobate hinge rivetted to it. From the *lorica*, possibly part of a shoulder piece. (6) Embossed bronze stud with niello inlay; probably from a harness leather.

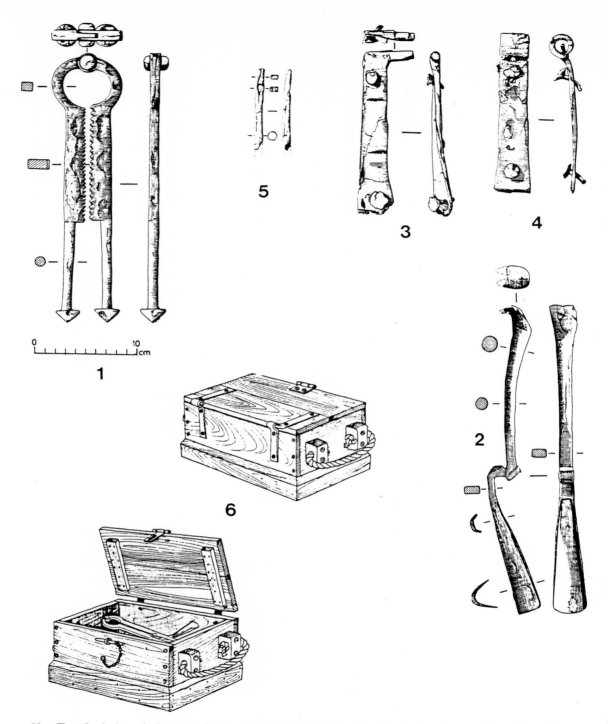

63. Two farrier's tools from the Cattlemarket. Scale: approx. 1/3. (1) A pair of emasculators for gelding cattle and horses. (2) Farrier's 'buttrice' for shaping horses' hooves. (3) & (4) Two parts of a hinge from a box. (5) Linch pin for securing box. (6) Conjectural reconstruction of box.

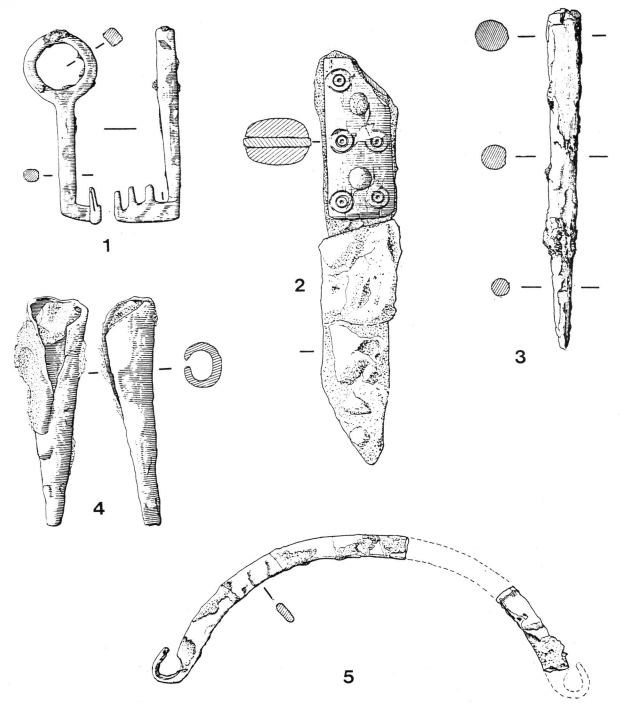

64.   Iron objects from the Cattlemarket. (1) Key, approx. full size. (2) Knife with bone handle with ring-dot decoration, full size. (3) Iron punch. Scale: 1/2. (4) Ploughshare tip, Scale: 1/2. (5) Bucket handle from a wooden bucket found at the bottom of a well. Scale: 1/2.

whistles, toggles and gaming counters. Leather workers have left no trace of their trade, but we may be sure that they were in the town, making belts, harnesses, buckets, jerkins, tents for the military and many other indispensable items in every-day use. The fact that the region was a wool-producing area points to cloth manufacture, and the fulling of cloth to clean and thicken it is a process that can sometimes be recognised by archaeologists. So far, the only possible site is below the Council Offices at East Pallant House, where Dr. Wilson found four square-cut pits[9] which had been lined, one with timber and the others with cement. One pit had a deposit of fullers earth, which heightens the possibility that this was the remains of a small fulling mill.

Stoneworking must have been an important local industry. The local stones most suitable for building purposes (apart from flint) were greensand and the ferruginous sandstone which outcrops near Midhurst; a quarry is known at Lodsworth. A large number of hand querns used for grinding corn have been found in and near to Chichester, especially on the Cattlemarket site, in contexts dating from the late first century onwards and most of these can be identified as coming from Lodsworth. Apart from querns, small mortars, basins, frame mouldings and other items of decorative stoneware were manufactured, the last four items usually being made from Sussex marble, a fossiliferous limestone similar to Purbeck marble. Large amounts of masons' 'offcuts' were found during the recent excavations east of Fishbourne Roman palace and many of these had been re-cut to form elements of an 'opus sectile' floor, while other rejects had been re-fashioned to make small whetstones. These were very important in Romano-British society. The need to maintain a good 'edge' on tools, knives and weapons meant that a whetstone was a very necessary item of equipment to carry around, which must be why so many of the smaller ones have a hole pierced through for suspension by a leather thong. Many of the locally produced hones were made from either a sandy limestone or a micaceous mudstone, but a fair proportion of those found in Chichester were imported from outside – an indication that the trade was an important one.

Other products of local stone quarries were large masonry items such as column drums, paving slabs and stone gutters. The remains of some of these can be seen at Fishbourne, where the later stone robbers left fragments of column bases and part of a stylobate and gutter in position. Other fragments have been found in Chichester at the south end of the Forum area, but only a very small fraction of the worked stone used in the public buildings now survives, the remainder having been robbed for later buildings.

The countryside

No study of Roman Chichester would be complete without taking a look at the countryside which it served. As the *civitas* capital, *Noviomagus Regnensium* was the administrative centre of a region which probably comprised all of Sussex and possibly part of eastern Hampshire. Northwards, the old capital of the northern Atrebates, *Calleva Atrebatum* (Silchester), would have served a region which included Surrey, part of northern Hampshire and southern Berkshire. Westwards, it is likely that *Venta Belgarum* (Winchester) administered the remainder of Hampshire and part of Wiltshire.

Noviomagus was not centrally placed within its territory and, although the requirements of government were met, it is likely that the more remote areas at the eastern end of the region developed their own market centres to serve local needs. Professor Cunliffe[10] has suggested that two might have been at Hassocks and Pulborough. However, it is with the coastal plain and the downland north of the city that we are most closely concerned, since the areas immediately adjacent to the town would most truly reflect the vicissitudes of urban life. For this reason the Chichester Excavations Committee for many years studied a region north of the town, based on the Chilgrove and West Dean valleys. More recently, the study has been extended to include the Mardens. Three Roman villas have been excavated and a study of the evolution of the landscape has been carried out. It has now been expanded to try and close the historical and archaeological 'gap' between the end of the Roman period and the establishment of the kingdom of the South Saxons.

We have already discussed (p. 20) a number of 'early' masonry villas in Sussex which might have belonged to some of the Atrebatic aristocracy but, for the most part, farming in late Iron Age Sussex was likely to have been mainly based on small peasant holdings, some of which carried on into the Roman period. A few of these have been identified, for example at Copse Farm, Oving,[11] and Hazel Road, Bognor Regis.[12] At Copse Farm, the focus of the Iron Age settlement appears to have moved to a new site which continued into the Roman period, but does not appear to have developed further. At other sites, continuity can be traced up to the fourth century, by which time the more successful had developed into prosperous and comfortable 'villas'.

West Sussex has always been prime farming country, no less in the Roman period than now, and one of the most striking features to emerge from the study of land use is the intensity of the farming activity especially during the fourth century. In the Chilgrove valley, where two villas have been completely excavated, field walking and aerial survey suggest that the number of farms in the late Roman period was pretty much what it was until a few years ago, before modern farming practice altered the balance in favour of large holdings. A similar situation was noted in the Darenth valley, near Dartford in Kent, where it was observed that Roman 'villas' occurred about every mile down the valley.

At Selsey, where the old Iron Age *oppidum* of Verica is presumed to have been, a large area has been eroded by the sea since the Roman period, but it can be seen from the find spots of Roman pottery recorded on the map (Pl. 22) that an extensive settlement must have existed there, served by a road which issued from the South gate at Chichester. A cremation cemetery is known at Grafton Road, where pottery was found during digging for drains in 1959 and a hoard of 975 Roman coins was found in the grounds of Halton House before World War Two. Near to the *Anchor Inn*, and now in the garden of a bungalow, a Roman well was found in 1962 which must have belonged to a nearby house, not yet discovered. Other finds of pottery and coins in Bracklesham and the Witterings indicate the presence of small settlements, but the only Roman masonry villa to be excavated on the coastal plain near to Selsey was at Sidlesham, where Dr Wilson dug the bath house in 1951.[13] Unfortunately, the excavations were not of the scope to answer many of the questions which pose themselves today, and the absence of a comprehensive pottery report which can be related to the stratigraphy means that the life-span of the villa can only be guessed at. It is possible that the villa economy may have been partly based on salt production, since it is very near the saltings, and salt extraction by the evaporation process was widely practised along the coast. However, intensive cultivation and urban development along the coastal belt during the last 70–80 years has destroyed much of the evidence for Roman and pre-Roman occupation and, with the exception of Dr. Wilson's work at Sidlesham, very little has been archaeologically excavated. In the main, all we are left with is a catalogue of finds and findspots, but these are so numerous that a picture of intensive land use can be built up, probably coupled with fishing and salt extraction on holdings near the shore line.

At Sidlesham, three periods of building were recognised by the excavator, the earliest one consisting of a ditched enclosure. This is claimed to be of first-century date but in the absence of any published pottery it should be treated with caution. The coin series goes on until the fourth century and it might well be, by analogy with the Chilgrove villas, that the masonry buildings date from the earlier part of that century.

Another villa has been discovered in the area of Tarrant Street, Arundel.[14] So far, it has only been possible to explore a small part of this building, but the excavator found two distinctive thin-walled hypocaust tiles which have been dated to the reign of Nero and which have been noted in one of the 'early' villas mentioned in Chapter 2. The Tarrant Street villa might, on this evidence, prove to be yet another example of a first-century masonry villa, but more excavation is needed to clarify this point. A villa or farm may exist at Densworth Farm, East Ashling, where a small cremation cemetery was discovered by the Revd. Henry Smith in 1857.[15] The burials, which included two in cists with others placed in the soil nearby, probably belonged to a farm in the vicinity. Trial excavations by J. Holmes in 1960,[16] following up a discovery of Roman pottery in a pipe trench, found the cemetery excavated by Smith but did not locate the buildings. Subsequently, building works near the farm buildings produced more Roman pottery[17] and it seems likely that the farm or villa may be below the present farmhouse and associated outbuildings.

At Fishbourne, the palace would certainly have been the centre of a large estate, the limits of which are unknown. It probably remained within the family of Cogidubnus after the king's death and, as time went on, there were a number of alterations to the main building, with the occupants using less of the available living quarters than before. Finally, in the late third century, after a disastrous fire, the north wing was destroyed and the building was progressively robbed for building stone, so that by the fourth century it was completely deserted. However, this is not to say that the land was not being farmed, although the rising of the sea level at that time might have meant that some arable was lost to the encroaching sea. Recent excavation by David Rudkin[18] south of the palace has revealed the foundations of a large aisled barn with at least one phase of rebuilding, which dates from the first century A.D. and appears to go on until the late third century. The barn is right beside the water's edge and the land there must have flooded at every high tide in the fourth century. The original Roman land surface can now be seen in section in the drainage ditches dug in recent years by the farmer. The old surface is covered by a layer of silt between 20 and 30 centimetres thick.

It seems certain that this building belonged to the palace estate and was used for a number of functions including corn drying, storage, and probably as living quarters for some of the estate workers, whether slave or free. The coin evidence indicates the same time-span as the main palace, and the only fourth-century coins found can be

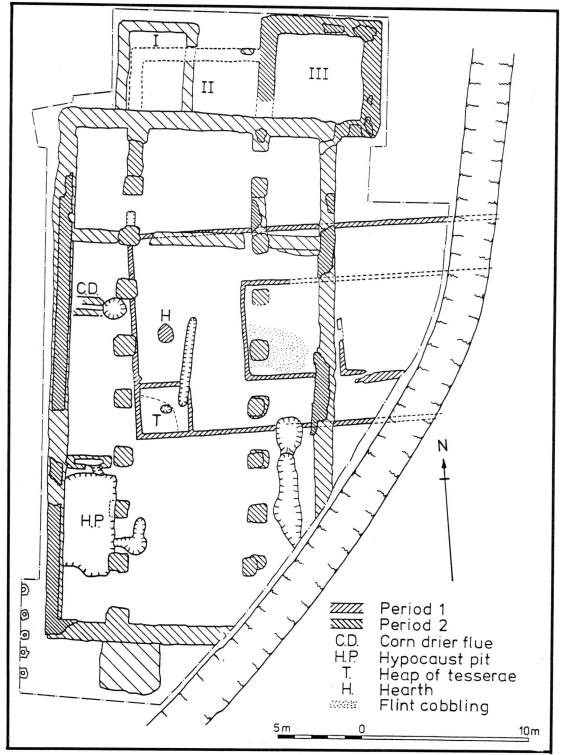

5m   0   10m

65. Plan of Roman building at Fishbourne creek, drawn by D.J. Rudkin.

attributed to later stone-robbing activities. It is likely that this barn would have been only one of a number located in various parts of the estate, but only sustained fieldwork and some luck will bring them to light. (Pl. 65)

Excavation to the east of the palace in 1985–6 in advance of the new Havant-Chichester trunk road has shown that there is an extensive semi-formal garden, probably in excess of five acres, on the eastern approach to the palace from the direction of Chichester (Pl. 66). A gravelled road, which must have branched off from the main road from Chichester, led straight to the palace entrance, and the area to the north of this road was laid out with gravelled paths, drainage ditches and ornamental waterways. Trees and shrubs were planted in bedding trenches, which were filled with manure dug from the many middens which must have been stacked up in the back areas of the palace grounds. The evidence from this excavation is still being studied but it seems likely that this part of the palace environs also ceased to function before the end of the third century as there is an absence of fourth-century coins from the site, only one being found in the topsoil.[19]

Further west, at Bosham (see p. 70), a large Roman building was found in 1882.[20] This has never been completely excavated and the account by the Revd. Mitchell

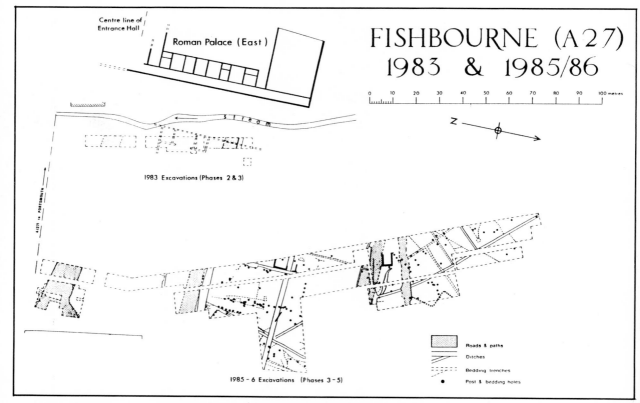

66.   Plan of excavations east of Fishbourne Roman Palace, showing part of a semi-formal garden or park.

leaves much to be desired. Whether it is a villa, with a bath house and mosaics or whether it is a temple, as E.W.Black suggests,[21] will have to await further investigation. It was reported by Mitchell that a coin of Honorius was found, built into one of the walls, which indicates that building, or re-building, was being carried out in the early fifth century. Two marble heads found in Bosham may be identified with this, or another site. They were both from private gardens, however, and could just as easily be collectors' items brought from Italy during the 18th or 19th centuries. Bosham is about four miles from Fishbourne and the building or buildings discussed here could well have originally been part of the palace estate. If it is a temple, then it might well mark the boundary of the palace estate.

Other sites are known at Kingsham and Whyke, nearer to the city, where burials and finds of coins and pottery point to estates just outside the city limits. Other Roman sites within a 10–mile radius of the *civitas* capital are shown in Pl. 22.

The downland

Work in the Chilgrove valley and at Upmarden from 1963 to 1977 has provided a good picture of the growth and decay of Romano-British farming from the early second to the early fifth century. The valley is six miles north of Chichester, alongside the road to Silchester, which runs over Heathbarn Down (Pl. 67), and passes within a few score metres of the second of the Chilgrove villas. The first to be excavated (Chilgrove 1) lies in the bottom of the valley on the east side of Bow Hill and occupies the same site as an earlier Iron Age homestead of the first century B.C. The villa, however, did not start until the late first or early second century A.D. It began as a single range of buildings, timber-framed on dwarf walls of flint construction, with a small stockyard for animals and surrounded by a palisade.[22] By the fourth century it had been re-built as a single range of masonry buildings with a bath-house at the south end. Mosaics were laid in two rooms and one had underfloor heating. By this time the stockyard

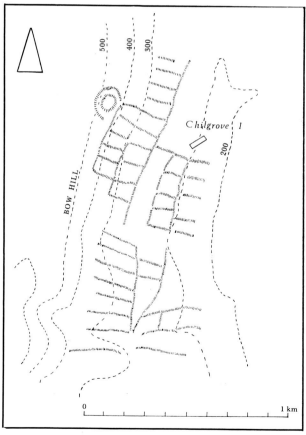

67. Iron Age field system around Chilgrove Roman Villa 1.

had been enlarged and a number of barns and domestic buildings were built within it, but a complete plan could not be recovered due to ploughing in recent times. The small rectangular fields to the south and east of the villa (Pls. 67–71) had been farmed in the Iron Age and seem to have continued in use throughout the Roman period. The total land under arable was of the order of 300 acres and probably about 15 to 20 people were needed to staff the farm. The evidence of the pottery and coins both from Chilgrove 1 and the other two villas shows that in the fourth century at least they were well able to afford luxury items such as fine pottery and glassware from Gaul and the Rhineland and jewellery of bronze, jet and silver. The principal crops raised by the farmers would have been wheat, oats and barley; peas, beans and a range of domestic vegetables would also figure on the list. The wheat varieties known to have been grown in the Iron Age and Roman periods were spelt (*Tr. spelta*) and emmer (*Tr. dicoccum*). Both of these varieties have been grown in modern times with modern wheat hybrids and some interesting yield factors have emerged. Experimental crops grown at Fishbourne Roman palace by the Butser Ancient Farm Project Trust in 1986[23] showed that both ancient wheat varieties out-performed the modern wheat, the weight per acre for each type being:

> Modern wheat 2.02 tons
> Spelt wheat 2.24 tons
> Emmer wheat 2.38 tons

A study of the animal bones from both Chilgrove villas showed that cattle and sheep were raised and eaten, but that few pigs were present. This may suggest either that pork was not very popular or, perhaps more likely, that most of the pigs went to market in Noviomagus. This is to some extent confirmed by a study of the large numbers of animal bones found at the Cattlemarket site outside the Eastgate, where the proportion of pig bones is higher than at Chilgrove, although still low compared with cattle and sheep. The abandoned food bones left in the stockyards of the villas and thrown into the wells and cess-pits represents only what was killed and eaten on the farm and we have no information about the numbers of cattle and other stock driven into the market at Chichester. It is likely that most of the taxes paid to the state and collected at Chichester were in the form of the *annona* or corn tax, with perhaps some part being paid in livestock, as the Roman army needed large amounts of cattle to provide meat and lard and hides for tents and leather equipment.

Sheep seem to have increased in importance between the second and fourth centuries. At Chilgrove, sheep bones seem to form a larger proportion of the total in the fourth century and the same trend is perceptible at the Cattlemarket. It might indicate a switch in emphasis from arable to sheep at a time when less labour-intensive farming methods were being employed to counteract the shortage of manpower experienced during the fourth century. At the Cattlemarket, Levitan[24] has noted a steady increase in the size of the sheep from the first to the fourth century which he attributes to a deliberate policy of improvement on the part of the stockbreeders. A comparison with the sheep bones from Chilgrove shows that these were also of the 'improved' breed.

For the greater part of the life of Chilgrove 1 – from the early second century to the late third, it was a small timber-framed dwelling with a small stockyard and barn. The expansion came in the early fourth century when stability returned with the rule of the Emperor Constantine after a long period of unrest and civil disturbance. It seems

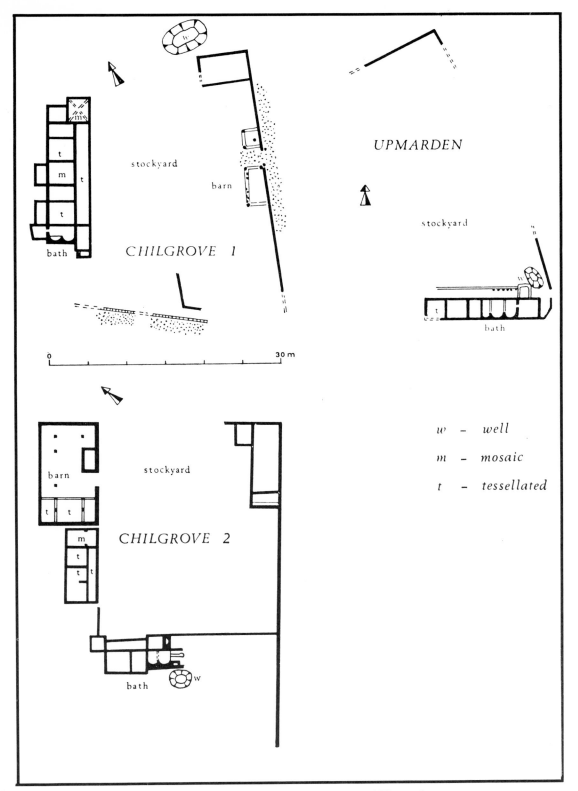

UPMARDEN

stockyard

bath

stockyard

barn

bath

CHILGROVE 1

0   30 m

barn

stockyard

CHILGROVE 2

bath

w – well

m – mosaic

t – tessellated

68. Plans of Roman villas at Chilgrove and Upmarden.

69. Chilgrove 1: cleaning the mosaic in Room 6 before raising it.

70. Chilgrove 1: the bath suite, looking east.

71. Chilgrove 1: reconstruction of fourth-century villa (by C. de la Nougerede).

72. Chilgrove 1: the Period 4 mosaic in Room 6 (drawn by C. de la Nougerede).

that the period of prosperity may have lasted until the 360s and then the farm lapsed into decay. Part of the main building suffered badly from a fire, and the bath-house went out of use and was finally dismantled and backfilled. The latest coins from the site are those of Magnentius (A.D. 363), and the absence of coins of Valentinian I, which are normally prolific on fourth-century sites, suggests that the villa was not then occupied by people using money. However, there is evidence that the land was still being worked, as corn-drying ovens were in use in a barn in the stockyard; an iron-working furnace was built upon a tessellated floor in one of the rooms, and large amounts of iron tools, fittings, nails and needles were being manufactured. Since the villa was too far from Noviomagus, which in any event had iron working industries outside the walls, it follows that the tools were being made for every-day use on the farms. By this time, most of the rooms were open to the sky, although one room had a central post inserted which supported a makeshift roof where the workers probably sheltered. Someone had dug a hole in one corner and buried a baby in it, while in the next room an amphora had been inserted into the floor either as a storage container or a urinal.

It is not known for how long this period of semi-dereliction lasted before the villa was finally abandoned; the absence of any dateable pottery of the sub-Roman period and the resumption of a barter economy after nearly four centuries of Roman rule makes the end-point impossible to conjecture. It seems very likely, however, that Chilgrove 1 became amalgamated with Chilgrove 2, possibly at some time in the 360s and that from then onwards most or all of the farm staff were billeted at Chilgrove 2.

Chilgrove 2 developed on almost parallel lines with Chilgrove I a mile away, although there was no Iron Age settlement nearby. In the second century it was a small, single range of rooms of timber-framed construction, with the stockyard contained within a ditched enclosure. It developed slowly until the early fourth century when it was rebuilt on the same plan as before but with wide masonry footings which probably supported a half-timbered building. A large aisled barn was built on to the north end and a bath suite was constructed at right-angles to the original range of rooms. The ditch around the original stockyard was filled in and replaced by a masonry wall with barns built along the inside. Thus, unlike Chilgrove 1, it developed into a courtyard villa if the barns are included (Pl. 68). Later on, the aisled barn at the north end had living quarters built in at the south end and one room was floored with a tessellated pavement with a unique design incorporating nine crude circles (Pl. 73). Probably at the same time, the original range of rooms was modified and a mosaic was laid in the principal room. Unfortunately, this did not survive the plough and we only know of it from the loose tesserae in the ploughsoil. (Pls. 74 & 75)

At some time after the mid-fourth century, probably at the same time that the first Chilgrove villa was undergoing the transition from comfortable villa to semi-derelict ruin, the aisled barn at Chilgrove 2 was drastically altered. One of the three rooms at the end was dismantled, the centre part of the roof removed and a series of domestic ovens were cut into the floor. Later on, a large bread oven was built against the inside of the west wall and the size of the oven suggests that it was intended to supply the needs of an increased labour force, some of whom may have worked the land at Chilgrove 1.

If the two villas *were* amalgamated (with perhaps others in the valley), we should

73. Chilgrove 2: Building 2, Room 7, looking south.

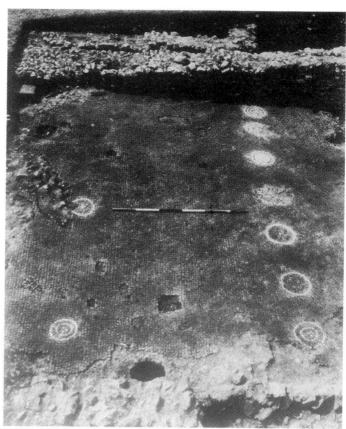

74. Chilgrove 2: south-east wing and bath house.

75.   Chilgrove 2: Period 4, reconstruction by C. de la Nougerede.

look for reasons why it happened. It might be that the owners had sold up and gone elsewhere to live, away from the hazards of fourth-century life near the coast, constantly raided by Saxon pirates, or that the land was being worked for absentee owners by bailiffs. But perhaps the picture of wealthy owners fleeing from Saxon raids and banditry is too dramatic and there may be a more mundane explanation. Internal conflict, plague and a falling birthrate had combined to produce a serious shortage of manpower in Britain and Gaul and this must have meant that in many areas land went out of cultivation because there were not enough people to work the soil. Animal husbandry, before the invention of tractors and mechanical methods of harvesting, was much less labour intensive than arable farming and the amalgamation of a number of small farming units in the valley might be due to a switch in farming practice, possibly with the emphasis upon sheep. Combining a number of farms in these circumstances would mean a number of redundant farm buildings and labourers would have to be re-deployed. Some of the spare buildings would be adapted to other uses and others would rapidly deteriorate without proper maintenance.

At Chilgrove 2 the coin sequence goes on until Valentinian I, about eleven years later than Chilgrove 1 and, like that villa, the only pottery that can be identified with confidence is the late fourth-century wares from the Oxford and New Forest kilns. Eventually part of the villa, in this case the large aisled barn, caught fire. The roof tiles of Horsham stone fell across the floors, beams smouldered on the tesssellated pavements and the partition walls between the rooms collapsed above them. But this did not signify the end of habitation. Although the barn was not rebuilt, someone went in after the fire and cleared away part of the rubble from the floor with circle designs on it and salvaged some of the less badly burnt beams, possibly for use elsewhere on the farm. Whatever the reason, a number of nails were extracted and left in two heaps on the floor.

The bath-house had been modified at some time after the mid-fourth century and it is possible that the *caldarium* or hot room, together with the stoke-hole, had been adapted for corn-drying, with charcoal being used as the fuel. Here, as at Chilgrove 1, in the last stages of occupation there are hearths built upon floors, makeshift roofs set over rooms with a centrally placed post dug through earlier floors, indicating that people were living (perhaps squatting would be a better term) in buildings which had become run down and abandoned.

The question which poses itself is, 'Where did the people go?'. At some time, probably in the late fourth century, but perhaps even later, the villas ceased to be occupied, even on a 'squatter' basis, but whether the land continued to be worked is open to conjecture. It might well be that the last generation of farm workers were then living in nearby villages, still working some of the land and using the old villa buildings for wintering their stock. By then, much of the land would have reverted to scrub and, with a population that was still in decline, the reversion would increase as time went on, with the peasants only growing enough for themselves, having no incentive to produce for a market.

Much less is known about the third villa at Pitlands Farm, Upmarden. It was only possible to excavate the wings which contained the baths, the remainder of the villa being below the 17th-century farmhouse and farm buildings. Here, the archaeological evidence indicates that the bath block was built at some time after the late third century and the standard of building was, if anything, slightly better than that at the Chilgrove villas. The site was again occupied during the late Saxon period and has been a farm ever since.[25] Another villa is known, not far away at West Marden. This was discovered in 1895 and Dr. Talfourd Ely carried out some excavations there in 1907 and 1910. Further work was done by S.E.Winbolt in 1924 and a plan was produced which was re-published by the present writer in 1979. More recently, work carried out by the County Archaeologist, Fred Aldsworth, under the auspices of a Manpower Services Commission scheme to landscape and preserve the site, has enabled a reinterpretation to be made, and five phases of development to be worked out (Pl. 76).[26] It can be seen that this villa also started as a three-roomed structure and later developed into a corridor building with a rather odd circular room at the end. This was removed in the next phase when the villa was again enlarged and finally, in the fifth phase, the original three-roomed building had become a nine-roomed corridor villa with another square building constructed at the west end, connected to the villa by a curtain wall. The full extent of the villa and its outbuildings has not been established, although it is hoped that further landscaping work may provide more information.

At Bignor, perhaps the most famous of the Sussex villas, much less is known about the development and decline, due to its discovery and excavation in the early 19th

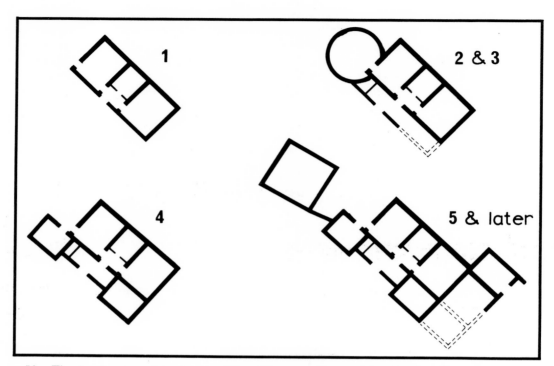

76.   The development of the Roman villa at Watergate Hanger, West Marden. Phases 1–5 (after F. G. Aldsworth).

century, when less consideration was given to these factors than would be the case today. The villa was excavated by Samuel Lysons who produced a plan and drawings of the mosaics (Pl. 77). The mosaics were roofed in by the owners and have been on display to the public ever since. Subsequent work on the villa by Frere in 1956 and 1962,[27] Aldsworth in 1983[28] and Aldsworth and Rudling in 1985[29] has to some extent remedied the deficiencies in Lyson's work and produced a more accurate plan (Pl. 78).

Frere's work shows that there was some Iron Age occupation, or at least cultivation of part of the site, and a Romano-British farm seems to have been established by the end of the first century A.D. A timber-framed building was constructed at the end of the second century and this was succeeded, after a fire, by a four-roomed stone building. Thereafter there were a number of alterations and additions during the second half of the third century. At the end of the third century, as with the Chilgrove villas, there was a dramatic expansion, with the earlier house being re-built and the north and south wings added and, later in the fourth century, more rooms were added to the north wing and the mosaics laid.

On the east side of the courtyard villa in the fourth century was a large stockyard with at least four buildings which are identified as barns, but it is not known whether they are all contemporary or whether the two buildings in the north-east and south-east corners replaced the other two (Pl. 78). Professor Applebaum,[30] assuming that the four buildings were all in use at the same time, calculated that there was room for

77. (*right*) S. Lysons' drawing of the Bignor mosaic, 'Winter'.

78. (*below*) Bignor Roman Villa (after F. G. Aldsworth).

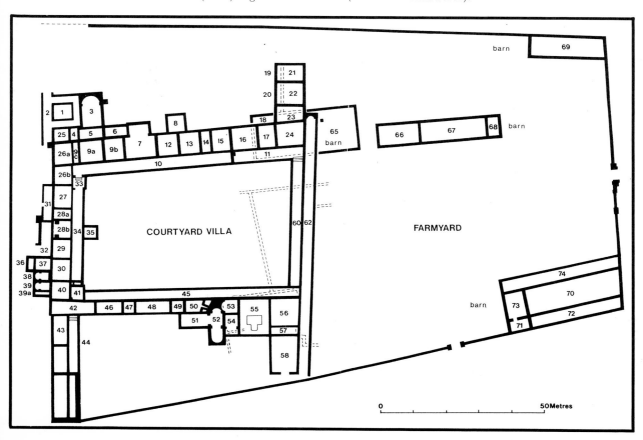

wintering 197 sheep, 12 teams of oxen (two oxen per team) and 55 other cattle. Applebaum also calculated (based on 12 plough teams) that, given a three-field system of crop rotation, the Bignor farmers could plough 732 acres in 292 work days per year, due allowance being made for the difference in ploughing rates between light and heavy soils.

The rapid expansion of the villa in the fourth century has prompted some discussion as to whether it was the home of a single wealthy family or whether, as E.W.Black suggests,[31] the building was occupied by three families, one in the west wing and two in the north. This can never be proved but, whatever the situation was, there is little doubt that the luxurious and well-appointed villa was based, in part at least, on the highly prosperous estate which surrounded it and which may have been in excess of 2000 acres. Applebaum noted (*op. cit.* p. 119) that the majority of animal bones recovered during excavation were of sheep and it would be interesting if they could be compared with the bones from the Cattlemarket at Chichester and those from the Chilgrove villas to establish whether they too were of the 'improved' breed.

The site of another villa is known nearby, at Duncton, where the bath-house was excavated in the 19th century.[32] The remainder of the villa buildings were not located and there is no evidence for the date of construction. On analogy with Bignor and the Chilgrove villas, the masonry bath-house might also date to the late third or early fourth century. The proximity of the site to the Bignor villa poses the question whether Duncton in the fourth century had amalgamated with its larger neighbour, perhaps as part of a general rationalisation of farming practice to maximise production – particularly of sheep and woollen products – in response to the demands of an expanding market. If this proved to be the case, then it would go a long way towards explaining the expansion of Bignor as a super 'home farm' fringed by satellite farms, either taken over completely or run by bailiffs. This is no more than a possibility which has already been noted in the Chilgrove valley and where it is a matter of recorded history that modern farming practice has followed the same path over the same land.[33] Considerable fieldwork is needed, first to locate other possible villa sites in the vicinity and then to carefully excavate them to study the complete cycle of origin, development and decay.

The pattern which emerges from the small sample of downland villas we have looked at seems to be remarkably consistent. Apart from the 'early' villas with first-century features mentioned above, it appears that a significant number started life as modest farms and remained that way until the late third or early fourth century, when for some reason there was a big expansion in agriculture, with the farmers producing and selling enough surplus to be able to afford luxury building. Not all farms made it into the big league. Some remained as peasant holdings, as they had been in the late Iron Age, but these were probably on marginal land. It is likely that small, one-family units were as much a part of the Romano-British landscape in the third century as they were in the first, but the remains of these small settlements are usually difficult to identify after centuries of ploughing. The big expansion in agriculture and the corresponding rise in the material wealth of the farmers in the fourth century indicates a big increase in the market available to the producers. The troubles and upheavals of the third century have already been mentioned. Following the restoration of Roman rule by Constantius in 296 there must have been an increase in business confidence and an expansion of trade. In Chichester there is evidence for a renewal of building activity[34] and this might reflect the needs of a growing urban population, with a corresponding increase in the market served by the local farms. In view of the handsome profits being made this may not be the complete picture and there must have been other factors. One might be that more of the produce was going abroad and that, as in later centuries, wool and woollen goods were high on the list. It is possible that the mosaics at Bignor and Chilgrove might have been partly subsidised by the wool from the backs of the sheep grazing on the Downs. There is a small pointer in this direction in a price-fixing edict by Diocletian in A.D. 301 when two British woollen items, the *Birrus Britannicus* (a type of hooded duffle coat) and the *Tapete Britannicus* (a woollen rug which could be used as a saddlecloth) were mentioned. Corn was also being exported to the Continent in the fourth century – there is a record of 600 bargeloads being sent to the Rhineland in 359 but, after allowing for these factors, it is likely that the most important element in the prosperity of Britain at that time was, as Professor Frere suggests,[35] the fact that Britain enjoyed a favourable balance of trade. In the early years of the province there had been very heavy capital investment by businessmen from Italy and Gaul, and the loans had to be repaid, often at very high rates of interest. In addition, much of the luxury tableware and other prestige goods were being imported from Gaul and the Rhineland. By the fourth century, as Frere points out, the debt burden had been cleared, manufacturing industry was in local hands and Britain could export a surplus of agricultural products.

Chapter Six

Sub-Roman to Saxon

The change in status from a prosperous, late Roman *civitas* capital to a decaying sub-Roman town in the mid-late fifth century took place against a background of strife and dissension within the Empire, exacerbated by barbarian raids and invasion. In 367 what became known as 'the great barbarian conspiracy' took place when Picts, Scots and Attecotti, apparently acting together for the first time, attacked Britain, while the Franks and Saxons swept down upon Gaul. In Britain, the northern defences were overrun, the Count of the Saxon Shore was killed and the *dux Britanniorum*, the military commander of the land-based forces, was taken prisoner. Civil rule appears to have broken down completely and something approaching anarchy resulted over the greater part of the country.

Order was restored the following year by Count Theodosius, who landed with detachments of the regular army and eventually brought the province back under Roman rule. Theodosius carried out a thorough and far-reaching reorganisation of the defences of the province, especially of the northern frontier and the Saxon Shore forts around the east and south-east coasts. The addition of the bastions to the Chichester defences probably dates from this time. For a short while after this Britain enjoyed a high level of prosperity, but the growing threat to the Empire by barbarian forces put an increasing strain on the depleted numbers of regular troops available to meet it. The situation was made worse by the ambitions of usurper Emperors in Britain who, in 383 and 407, took large armies abroad to fight for their claim to the purple. These adventures seriously weakened the forces in Britain and few, if any, of the troops returned. By 410 it is likely that no regular detachments of the Roman army remained in the province and, when the Saxon raids began again (a particularly serious raid was recorded in that year), the people of Britain were left to organise their own defences.

In order to understand what happened in Chichester at the end of the Roman occupation it is necessary to look at what documentary sources there are and try to reconcile them with the slight archaeological evidence that we have. By 410 the legions had gone and the Emperor Honorius wrote to the towns of Britain telling them to look after their own defences. This may have been no more than the admission that Roman rule in Britain had ended, thus giving the citizens the right to take up arms for their own defence, and legalising a situation which had probably existed for some time. Commenting on this in the sixth century, *Zozimus* (IV.5) wrote, 'The Britons took up arms and, braving danger for their own independence, freed their cities from the barbarians threatening them; and all Armorica [Brittany] and the other provinces of Gaul copied the British example and freed themselves in the same way, expelling their Roman governors and establishing a state of their own as best they could'.

This reference by Zozimus to the Britons and Gauls expelling their Roman governors may mean that the old central government, already completely discredited, had been overthrown by local factions determined to take over their own government and defence.

It also indicates that there were two parties within the province, one pro-Roman and the other representing an emerging nationalism, and in the end these divisions were to prove fatal in the face of the threat from the barbarians. Procopius (*de bello Vandalico i, 2, 38*) writing at some time in the mid-sixth century stated, 'that from now on, Britain was ruled by tyrants' (i.e. overlords). It is likely that their territories were based on local strongpoints and these may have been the old *civitas* capitals with their strong walls, some of the Iron Age hill-forts, the forts of the Saxon shore and, in some instances, the large estates where the owners were sufficiently wealthy to maintain armed forces. About 430, Vortigern, who appears to have emerged as the high king or overlord of Britain, or at least part of it, brought in Saxon mercenaries led by Hengist and Horsa to protect key areas along the shores of Britain against the Picts and Scots. By this time the manpower situation in Britain must have been desperate, following outbreaks of plague and a general decline in the population due to a falling birth rate, and in bringing in the Saxons and Jutes to fight for him Vortigern was following the well-established Roman policy of hiring mercenaries and interposing them as buffer defences in exchange for grants of land.

At first the policy worked well, and Hengist and Horsa defeated the Picts, but they later rebelled against Vortigern and eventually he was forced to cede Kent and Sussex to Hengist. Vortigern is thought to have died soon after 458 and thereafter resistance to the Saxons appears to have passed to the 'Roman' party under forces led by Ambrosius and, later, by the legendary Arthur. The Saxons in the south-eastern settlements were totally defeated at the battle of Mons Badonicus (thought to be near Bath) c. 494 and for nearly 70 years they were contained within their boundaries. However, helped by divisions amongst the British, the Saxons again broke out from their lands in the early sixth century and less than a century later they were virtually in control of the whole of Britain excluding Cornwall, Wales and the kingdom of Strathclyde. This is the broad picture as far as we can see it, and against this backcloth we have to try and work to the fate of Noviomagus and the people living in the countryside around it.

Within the town the decline seems to start at some time after the third quarter of the fourth century. There is now evidence from recent excavations in Chapel Street to show that the large house on the north side of the cross-roads (House 2) was not enlarged to its final form until some time after the mid-fourth century,[1] and the latest date suggested for the large baulks of timber recovered from the cistern of the public baths in Tower Street is c. 370, according to the tree-ring dating which is to some extent confirmed by radio-carbon dating. These baulks of timber were probably part of the superstructure of the pumping equipment for the baths and, since the dates suggested are those when the trees from which the timbers were fashioned were cut down, the implication is that at some time in the 370s, if not later, the public baths were still functioning and equipment was being replaced.

A study of the latest Roman levels in the town seems to indicate that the decay was a slow process. There are signs in House 1, south of the Chapel Street crossroads (Pl. 79), of the rooms being sub-divided by wattle partitions and, in both House 1 and House 2, hearths were found built upon tessellated floors. A thick layer of organic silt accumulated above the rutted and pot-holed street nearby, and the public sewers running along the north side of the public baths and below County Hall gradually

79.   Late or sub-Roman hearth laid against a wall, later robbed.

silted up, with the wooden revetments collapsing. At the site of the Roman house at the rear of Mothercare (formerly David Greig),[2] now the central car park north of St. Andrew Oxmarket, roof tiles were found shattered where they had fallen on the floor below. Nowhere was there any sign of destruction by fire, but extensive robbing of Roman buildings for masonry to build the medieval town has in any case tended to blur the picture.

Outside the Eastgate, the suburb appears to have been deserted by the late fourth or early fifth century. One of the Roman wells excavated on the Needlemakers site in 1976 had been backfilled with rubbish from the settlement and amongst it was a number of coins of Valens (364–376)[3] and a small group of coarse black pottery grogged with sand and chalk. This type of pottery has been noted elsewhere on late Roman sites (e.g. Chilgrove 1 and 2) and may be locally-made wares which replaced the more sophisticated fabrics supplied by the large pottery industry at Alice Holt, near Farnham. The site subsequently became part of the inhumation cemetery discussed in Chapter 4 which probably continued to be used well into the fifth century. At the Cattlemarket, which is slightly nearer to the walls, the latest coins recovered from the bottom of well 3, which was functioning right up to the end of recorded activity on the site, were of the same date as those in the Needlemakers.

The problems for the archaeologist attempting to study Romano-British society in decline are considerable. The bronze coinage, which is prolific and represents total coin loss at the end of a money economy, can only take us as far as the last coin to be minted. Thereafter there is a time lag for the coin to reach the site, to be used and eventually lost or discarded, and we do not know how long it was after the last coin issues reached Chichester before a money economy was finally abandoned.

It is not possible to date closely the latest pottery found in the town, since after the collapse of the money economy there were no fine table wares reaching the area from the great pottery manufacturing centres at Oxford, the New Forest and Alice Holt. As the use of money gradually tailed off, it is likely that locally based enterprises would spring up to capture the market and there are a number of imitation fine red wares found in the district which cannot be assigned to the larger industries because the fabric is different. However, these local industries would have had a short life when barter became the accepted method of trading, but there is no way of knowing when this was. As far as present knowledge goes, the coin series within the town ends about seven years before the end of the fourth century, the latest issue being of Valentinian II (375–392). There are two exceptions. The first is a gold *solidus* of Valentinian III, which dates between 425 and 455. This was found in St. Pancras by a workman many years ago and no details of the find-spot or its associations are known. The coin, which is actually a Visigothic copy of a regular issue, is in mint condition and may never have circulated, possibly being held as 'bullion' by a trader against one of the occasions when goods coming in from outside the region might have to be paid for in cash. In such circumstances, 'cash' would always mean gold or silver, the bronze currency having no intrinsic value. The second exception is a bronze coin of Arcadius found in the topsoil in the Cattlemarket which dates to A.D. 408.

Although cut off from later supplies of coins from the Imperial mints, the bronze coinage may have continued in use for many years, being used less and less for transactions as society reverted to a more primitive lifestyle. In that society, specialists such as potters, local officialdom and tradesmen would be squeezed out as people became more and more self-sufficient at a lower level of subsistence. The farmers would be better off than their contemporaries in the towns. Being primary producers they could still feed themselves and bring their surpluses to market and barter for goods they needed, while townspeople would find themselves having to cultivate more and more of the land inside and outside the town in order to eat. Having reached the stage where it paid no-one to make pottery and market it, it would once again be made within the family group as it had been 400 years before.

During this period, when the town was turning in on itself and some of the land on the farms was going out of cultivation, there must have been changes in the ownership of some of the larger estates around Chichester. We have seen how the Chilgrove villas declined towards the end of the fourth century, with the farms probably being amalgamated but with the land still being worked, albeit in the absence of the former owners. Nearer to the town it is likely that the fields just outside the walls would have become increasingly important to the economy. The town might still have functioned as the local market, but it would have been on a much reduced scale as the farms reverted to subsistence level.

In the medieval period, the common fields belonging to the town were the Portfield and Guildenfield outside the East gate, with the Dean's Farm on the south and west and arable land belonging to the Bishop on the west and north sides. Many townsfolk held strips in the common fields, some of which survived until the enclosures in the 19th century. A glance at the Gardner Map of 1769 (Pl. 38) shows the skeleton of the Roman city still showing beneath the Saxon and medieval towns superimposed upon it, with the old Roman roads, no longer as straight as they once were, radiating out from the town gates. Between the roads, the field boundaries spread outwards like a spider's web.

Up to the 18th century and, in some instances much later, there was very little movement of land boundaries within the town limits or outside them. The present Chichester street plan derives from late Saxon town planning, which in turn was influenced by the Roman street plan. Outside the walls, the development of new tracks and the diversion of parts of the Roman roads to link up with newly developing Saxon settlements would distort the pattern of the sub-Roman countryside somewhat, but the fields nearest the walls would be unaffected by this. When we look at the Gardner Map, what we see is a palimpsest, with the 18th-century town and town fields little changed from early medieval times, and glimpses of the late Roman town and extra-mural settlements below. The pattern of the medieval common fields might well follow the boundaries of the town fields of the sub-Roman city. Up to the middle of the fifth century it is likely that organised life within the town was still vigorous, with enough men to form a militia to man the defences and operate the ballistae mounted on the bastions. There may still have been seaborne trade along the coast and across the Channel for a while, and if part of the garrison was mounted it would have provided a powerful defence against the raids of bandits and Saxon pirates upon the countryside. It is impossible to say how long this state of affairs might have lasted, but some speculation is permissible, based on what sparse documentary sources there are and a consideration of the (largely negative) archaeological evidence.

The coming of Aelle

The Anglo-Saxon Chronicle for 477 reads 'In this year Aelle came to Britain with his three sons Cymen, Wlencing and Cissa with three ships at the place which is called *Cymenesora* and there slew many Welsh and drove some to flight into the wood which is called Andredsleag'. There are two other entries relating to Aelle and Sussex, the second in 485, when Aelle fought against the Welsh near the bank of (the stream) *Mearcraedesburna* (possibly 'the river agreed by treaty'), and again in 491 when . . . 'In this year Aelle and Cissa besieged Andredescaster (the Saxon shore fort of Anderida [Pevensey]), and there slew all the inhabitants, there was not even one Briton left there'. It is now generally agreed by historians that the dates in this part of the Chronicle are 20 years too late, and 477 should therefore be 457, with Anderida being taken in 471. The place where Aelle landed has hitherto been thought to be the site of the Owers rocks to the south of Selsey Bill, which was then part of the mainland, but there is an inconsistency here as the 'Welsh' survivors of the encounter are said to have fled to the wood called Andredsleag (i.e. the Weald) which is many miles away from Selsey Bill. *Cymenesora* is mentioned in a later seventh-century charter and was thought to be in the neighbourhood of Selsey Bill, but Dr Martin Welch[4] points out that this may well be incorrect as the charter is a copy of a forgery. He suggests a site in East Sussex for Aelle's landing and, in view of later events and the account of the survivors of the first encounter fleeing into the Weald, it seems a feasible alternative. A landing near Selsey would in any case have been well within the orbit of any garrison at Chichester and it would have been to Chichester that any survivors would have fled.

If, then, the scene of Aelle's landing is transferred to East Sussex, the Chronicle's account of the Welsh fleeing to the Weald after the battle becomes more consistent with the geography. The next entry is in 485 (465) and refers to a battle on the banks of a river and may represent an attempt by Aelle to break out from an area delimited by treaty. It seems to have been an inconclusive encounter, as the Chronicle does not claim the victory for Aelle. Later on, in 491 (471) Aelle and Cissa appear to have raised a large enough force to besiege and take the fort of Anderida. This was a considerable achievement for a Saxon war leader and one wonders how it was carried out. Perhaps a sudden, swift attack which took the defenders by surprise, or perhaps a simultaneous onslaught by land and sea. The Chronicle is silent on the details and we shall never know how it was achieved, but there must have been compelling strategic reasons why Aelle thought it necessary to risk incurring heavy losses against a strongpoint like Pevensey. The advantage might be to deny to the British a harbour for a fleet which would be capable of harassing the Saxons, and perhaps the fort contained a force of cavalry which made attempts at permanent settlement dangerous. If the theory that Aelle landed in East Sussex is correct, then any attempt by him to move westwards would be under threat from his southern flank and this would be perhaps the most powerful reason for his campaign. On the other hand, the population within Anderida might have declined to a point when there were not enough men to man the walls, when a swift, opportunistic attack by Aelle could pen them within a trap. Whatever the circumstances, it is recorded as a victory for Aelle and one in which the defenders were given no quarter.

There is nothing in the Chronicle which refers to the western part of Sussex or to the old *civitas* capital of Noviomagus, and in considering the fate of the town we can only note this curious absence of comment and look to other sources for some clues as to what happened. The archaeological record is completely blank; after 25 years of almost continuous excavation within the town there is no evidence pointing to pagan Saxon occupation. The nearest cemetery where fifth-century Saxon burials are known is at Highdown Hill near Worthing, and other fifth-century cemeteries are known in East Sussex in the Bishopstone, Selmeston and Alfriston areas. Pagan Saxon occupation of the old Saxon shore fort at Porchester in Hampshire has also been demonstrated by Professor Cunliffe.[5] These cemeteries probably belong to the period when mercenaries were brought in to defend the Hampshire – Sussex coastline in the late fourth-early fifth centuries, when they were settled on blocks of land between the territories dominated by the Roman settlements at Chichester, Hassocks and Pevensey. None of these three areas shows any signs of fifth-century Saxon occupation or grave-goods, and as far as Chichester is concerned there is very little in the way of sixth-century material either. Only one item is known; a sixth-century brooch found at St. Pancras many years ago.

This had been repaired and had probably been in circulation for a long time before it was lost.

It is not until the late seventh century that we learn of the conversion of the South Saxons by St. Wilfrid. By then it is evident that the whole of the region had been settled by the Saxons and it is likely that the town was also occupied. Coarse, hand-made pottery, tempered with shell and chaff, very crude and underfired, is found as residual rubbish in later Saxon pits within the town, but no structures can be identified. The pottery could date as early as the seventh century and some of it is similar in fabric to the Pagham pot, now in Pagham church, which has been dated to the same period. The Pagham pot was found during grave-digging and it might be from an earlier, pagan Saxon cemetery largely destroyed by the Christian graveyard.

As far as the city of Chichester is concerned there is a gap in our knowledge which extends from some time after the middle of the fifth century to the late seventh. The difficulties of dating the terminal Roman phase of occupation have already been discussed, but if we assume that organised town life continued at least until the arrival of Aelle in 457, albeit at a low level, then we have to consider what impact his advent would have made. Fourteen years after his arrival he achieved a notable feat of arms in taking Anderida, but thereafter the Chronicle is silent about his activities. Had he gone on to take Chichester or even to force it to acknowledge his overlordship then it would almost certainly have been mentioned in the Chronicle. The absence of comment might imply that, for a time at least, Chichester was too strong to be taken, and no leader worth his salt would waste his men in attempts to subdue a fortress which was strategically less well placed than Anderida and which could be by-passed. With the rest of Sussex under Saxon domination Aelle could well afford to allow Chichester and the region around it to exist for a time as an enclave to be mopped up or absorbed at a later date.

Another possibility is that at that time the extreme western part of Sussex was within the area occupied by the British under Ambrosius. This model would also fit the negative evidence, but against it is the name of Chichester itself, *Cissa's castra*. It suggests that the town was the strong-point of Cissa, and the only Cissa we know of is the son of Aelle. Had Cissa taken the town it might be expected that some trace of pagan Saxon occupation would have come to light and, again, there is no mention in the Chronicle of such an event. Perhaps the explanation might be that Cissa, son of Aelle, claimed a nominal suzerainty over the town which was not recognised by the inhabitants; or perhaps by the last quarter of the fifth century the population within the walls had shrunk to a point where they no longer posed a military threat to the Saxons. We shall never know the true story, but if the model of a sub-Roman enclave at Chichester is about right for the period from Aelle's landing to the end of the fifth century, then there must have been a steady erosion of the peripheral territories by Saxon settlers during the early and middle sixth century. By then, they had filtered into the Mardens, ten miles north of Chichester, and the excavation of a hill-top cemetery near the Hampshire border from 1982 to 1987 (Pls. 80 & 81), has produced evidence to show that not only do the earliest burials date to the early sixth century, but that at least one of the inhabitants had Jutish connections.[6]

The work in the Mardens is not yet complete and the results will form part of another story – that of the growth of the kingdom of the South Saxons. The story of

80. Sixth-century pagan Saxon graves at Appledown,
Compton.

81. Jutish brooch from Grave 14 at Appledown.

Roman Chichester fades into obscurity a little before this. The end is impossible to determine in the absence of reliable documentary sources, and the discussion between historians and archaeologists continues, but the end probably came, not with fire and sword, but as the result of the gradual fusion of the local people with the newcomers.

THE DATES OF THE PRINCIPAL ROMAN EMPERORS AND THEIR CONTEMPORARIES IN BRITAIN AND GAUL

27 BC – AD 14.	Augustus		?c. 35–20 BC Commius
		Julio	
A.D.			?20 BC – AD 5 Tincommius
			?c. AD 10–42 Verica
14–37	Tiberius		? restored AD 43–5
		Claudian	
37–41	Gaius (Caligula)		
41–54	Claudius I		?45–85 Cogidubnus
54–68	Nero		
69–79	Vespasian		
79–81	Titus	Flavian	
81–96	Domitian		
96–98	Nerva		
98–117	Trajan		
117–138	Hadrian		
138–161	Antoninus Pius		
161–180	Marcus Aurelius	Antonine	
180–192	Commodus		
193–211	Severus		195–197 Clodius Albinus
211–217	Caracella		
		Severan	
218–222	Elagabalus		
222–235	Severus Alexander		
235–238	Maximinius I		
238–244	Gordian III		
244–249	Philip I		
253–260	Valerian I		*Gallic Emperors*
260–268	Gallienus		260–9 Posthumus
268–270	Claudius II		269–271 Victorinus
270–275	Aurelian		271–273 Tetricus
			British Emperors
284–305	Diocletian		287–293 Carausius
			293–296 Allectus
306–337	Constantine		
337–350	Constans		
337–361	Constantius II		
350–353	Magnentius		
361–363	Julian		
364–375	Valentinian		
364–378	Valens		
367–383	Gratian		383–388 Magnus Maximus
375–392	Valentinian II		
379–395	Theodosius I		
383–408	Arcadius		
395–423	Honorius		
425–455	Valentinian III		

References

Chapter One
1. A. Down, *Chichester Excavations 3* (1978), pp. 330–1.
2. See R. Bradley, 'A Field Survey of the Chichester Earthworks' in B.W. Cunliffe, 'Excavations at Fishbourne', vol. 1, *RRSAL* XXVI (1971), pp. 17–30.
3. E.C. Curwen, *The Archaeology of Sussex* (1954 ed.), p. 309.
4. See S.S. Frere, *Britannia* (1967), chapter 3 for an account of Caesar's expeditions.
5. Dio. LX, xix.1.
6. *Suetonius* Vesp. 4.
7. A. Down and M. Rule, *Chichester Excavations 1*, pp. 57–67.
8. A. Down, *Chichester Excavations 5* (1981), pp. 80–4.
9. A. Down, *Chichester Excavations 6* (1988).
10. A. Down, *Chichester Excavations 8* (forthcoming).
11. B.W. Cunliffe, 'Excavations at Fishbourne', vol. 1,, pp. 38–46 & Figs. 8 & 9, *RRSAL* XXVI (1971).
12. A. Down, 'Fishbourne 1983 & 1985/6'. See Chichester Excavations Committee Summary Reports for 1983/4 & 1985/6, also *Chichester Excavations 8* (forthcoming).
13. A. King, *Britannia* XI (1982), p. 142.

Chapter Two
1. A. Down, *Chichester Excavations 3*, pp. 56–8.
2. B.W. Cunliffe, *The Regni* (1973), pp. 74–82.
3. L. Scott, 'Angmering Roman Villa', *SAC* 79 (1938), pp. 3–44 & *SAC* 80 (1939), pp. 89–92.
4. S.E. Winbolt, 'The Roman Villa at Southwick', *SAC* 73 (1932), pp.13–32.
5. C.J. Praetorius, 'Paper on the Roman building near Pulborough, Sussex, *Proc. Soc. Antiq.*, vol. 23 (1910), pp.121–9.
6. J.E. Bogaers, 'King Cogidubnus: Another reading of RIB 91', *Britannia* X (1979).
7. A. Down, *Chichester Excavations 5*, p. 101 & Fig. 7.14.
8. E.W. Black, pers. comm.
9. A. Down, *Chichester Excavations 6* (1988).
10. M. Corney, 'A Field Survey of the Extra Mural region of Silchester', in M. Fulford, 'Silchester Defences, 1974–80', *Britannia Monograph Series* No. 5 (1984), pp. 287–8. See also M. Fulford, 'Calleva Atrebatum: an Interim Report on the excavation of the Oppidum, 1980–86', *PPS* 53 (in press).
11. G. Boon, *Archaeologia* 102 (1969), pp. 1–82.

Chapter Three
1. A. Down, *Chichester Excavations 5*, p. 48.
2. *SAC* 95, pp. 131–3.
3. *op. cit.*, pp. 131–2.
4. Dr. M. Henig, pers. comm.
5. A. Down and M. Rule, *Chichester Excavations 1*, pp. 127–38.
6. It is not clear from earlier references whether the floor found in the Bishop's garden is a mosaic or a plain tessellated floor or, indeed, whether both were found. *VCH*, vol. 3, p. 13 refers to 'much of a mosaic pavement'. J. Dallaway, *History of the Western Division of the County of Sussex*, vol. 1 (1815), p. 5 refers to a 'pavement', as does A. Hay, *The History of Chichester* (1804). The earliest reference is Camden's *Britannia*, where vol. 5, p. 489 mentions 'A curious piece of Roman pavement'.
7. A. Down, *Chichester Excavations 2*, p. 99 & Pl. 13.
8. *SAC* 100, pp. 93–9.
9. *Chichester Excavations Committee Summary Report for 1984/5. Chichester Excavations 8* (forthcoming).
10. A. Down, *Chichester Excavations 6* (1988).
11. A. Down and M. Rule, *Chichester Excavations 1*, pp. 165–71.
12. A. Down, *Chichester Excavations 5*, p. 67.

13. *op. cit.*, pp. 70–2.
14. *op. cit.*, p. 84.
15. J. Holmes, 'Chichester, the Roman town', *Chichester Papers* No. 50 (1965).
16. A. Down, *Chichester Excavations 3*, p. 86 & Fig. 7.20.
17. A. Down and M. Rule, *Chichester Excavations 1*, Figs. 5.10 & 5.11.
18. A. Down, *Chichester Excavations 5*, p. 70.
19. I.D. Margary, *Roman Roads in Britain* (1973).
20. Observations by Keith Lintott and others.
21. G.M. White, 'The Chichester Amphitheatre: Preliminary Excavations', *Ant. J.*, vol. 16, pp. 149–59.
22. A. Down and M. Rule, *Chichester Excavations 1*, pp. 19ff.
23. A. Down, *Chichester Excavations 8* (forthcoming).
24. J. Holmes, 'The Defences of Roman Chichester', *SAC* 100 (1962), pp. 80–92.
25. See S.S. Frere, 'British Urban Defences in Earthwork', *Britannia*, XV, pp. 663–74 for an up-to-date assessment.
26. A.E. Wilson, *SAC* 100 (1962), pp. 75–9.
27. A. Down, *Chichester Excavations 5*, pp. 41–4 & Figs. 5.16–5.18.
28. J. Holmes, *op. cit.*, pp. 84–6; A.E. Wilson, *SAC* 95 (1957), pp.125–7; A. Down, *Chichester Excavations 2*, pp. 59–71.
29. A. Down, 'The Orchard Street Bastion', *Chichester Excavations 6* (1988).
30. *Chichester Excavations Committee Summary Report for 1984/5.*

Chapter Four
1. Caesar, *The Conquest of Gaul.*
2. E.W. Black, 'The Roman Villas of South-East England', *BAR* British Series 171 (1987), pp. 29 and 75–6.
3. H. Barnes, 'The human skeletal remains from Eastgate Needlemakers', *Chichester Excavations 5*, pp. 117–18.
4. C. Wells, 'Romano-British Cemeteries at Cirencester: The Human burials', *Cirencester Excavations II* (1982), pp. 135–202.
5. M. Harman, 'The Anglo-Saxon burials from Appledown, Compton', in A. Down and M.G. Welch, *Chichester Excavations 7* (forthcoming).
6. A. Down and M. Rule, *Chichester Excavations 1*, pp. 53–126.
7. A. Down, *Chichester Excavations 3*, pp. 7–9.
8. A. Down, *Chichester Excavations 5*, Fig. 7.7.
9. *Chichester Excavations Committee Summary Report for 1985/6.*
10. *Gentleman's Magazine* (1830), Pt. 2.
11. *SAC* 80. pp. 171–92.
12. Down and Rule, *op. cit.*
13. J. Holmes, 'The Defences of Roman Chichester', *SAC* 100.
14. *SAC* 95, p. 130.
15. *op. cit.*, p. 131–3.
16. *op. cit.*, p. 131.
17. D.F. Allen, 'Did Adminius strike coins?', *Britannia* VII (1976), pp. 96–108.
18. M. Henig and D. Nash, 'Amminius and the Kingdom of Verica', *Oxford Journal of Archaeology*, vol. 1, no. 2 (1982), pp. 243–6.
19. A. Down, *Chichester Excavations 5*, p. 26.
20. A. McWhirr, *Roman Gloucestershire* (1981), p. 153.
21. A. King and G. Soffe, 'The Iron Age and Roman Temple at Hayling Island, Hants', *Britannia Monograph Series* (forthcoming).
22. *SAC* 18 (1866), pp. 1–3.
23. *SAC* 123 (1985), pp. 225–6 & Fig. 18.
24. See M.W.C. Hassall in *Chichester Excavations 5*, pp. 101–2.
25. M.W. Pitts, 'A Gazetteer of Roman sites', *SAC* 117 (1979), p.70 (7).

Note: I am grateful to Mr. E.W. Black for permission to reproduce his conjectural plan of the building at Bosham, which Mitchell refers to as having been discovered 'NW of Broadbridge House'.

REFERENCES

Chapter Five

1. B.W. Cunliffe, 'Relations between Britain and Gaul in the 1st century B.C.', in 'Cross Channel Trade between Gaul and Britain in the pre-Roman Iron Age', *Society of Antiquaries Occasional Paper* (New Series) IV (1984).
2. A. Down, 'Excavations at the Cattlemarket, Chichester', *Chichester Excavations 6* (1988).
3. A. Down, 'Excavations at the Theological College', *Chichester Excavations 8* (forthcoming).
4. A. Down, *Chichester Excavations 3*, Figs. 10.4 & 10.5.
5. D. Rudling *et al.*, 'The Excavation of a Roman Tilery on Great Cansiron Farm, Hartfield, Sussex', *Britannia* XVII (1986), pp.191–230.
6. T.K. Green, 'Roman Tileworks at Itchingfield', *SAC* 108 (1970), pp. 23–8.
7. A. Down, *Chichester Excavations 4*, Fig. 66.
8. A. Down, *Chichester Excavations 6* (1988); *Chichester Excavations 1*, pp. 143–7.
9. *SAC* 90, p. 167.
10. B.W. Cunliffe, *The Regni*, p. 73.
11. O. Bedwin and R. Holgate, 'Excavations at Copse Farm, Oving, Sussex', *PPS* 51 (1985), pp. 215–45.
12. O. Bedwin and M.W. Pitts, 'The excavation of an Iron Age settlement at North Bersted, Bognor Regis, West Sussex, 1975–6', *SAC* 116 (1978), pp. 293–346.
13. A.H. Collins, A.E. Wilson and C. Wilson, 'The Roman site at Sidlesham', *SAC* 111 (1973), pp. 2–19.
14. D. Rudling, 'Excavations in Tarrant Street, Arundel, West Sussex', *Bulletin of the Institute of Archaeology, University of London* (1984).
15. *SAC* 10, (1858), pp. 168–80.
16. *SNQ* (1961), pp. 242ff.
17. Mr. W. Sadler, pers. comm. The pottery is in the Chichester District Museum.
18. D.J. Rudkin, 'The excavation of a Romano-British site by Chichester Harbour, Fishbourne', *SAC* 124 (1986).
19. A. Down, 'Excavations at Fishbourne 1983 and 1985/6', *Chichester Excavations 8* (forthcoming).
20. H. Mitchell, 'On the early traditions of Bosham', *SAC* 18 (1866), pp. 1–3.
21. E.W. Black, 'The Roman buildings at Bosham', *SAC* 123 (1985), pp.255–6.
22. A. Down, *Chichester Excavations 4*, p. 43.
23. P.J. Reynolds, *Butser Ancient Farm Yearbook* (1986).
24. B. Levitan, 'The vertebrate remains from Chichester Cattlemarket', *Chichester Excavations 6* (1988).
25. A. Down, *Chichester Excavations 4*, pp. 101–8.
26. I am grateful to Mr. F.G. Aldsworth for kindly permitting me to reproduce his amended plan of the West Marden Villa.
27. S.S. Frere, 'Bignor Roman Villa', *Britannia* XIII (1982), pp.135–95.
28. F.G. Aldsworth, 'Bignor Roman Villa (The Baths): Excavations in 1985', (Interim Report, WSCC & English Heritage).
29. F.G. Aldsworth and D. Rudling, 'Bignor Roman Villa. Excavations in 1985: an Interim Report', WSCC.
30. S. Applebaum, 'Observations on the economy of the villa at Bignor', *Britannia* VI (1975), pp. 118–32.
31. E.W. Black, 'The Roman Villa at Bignor', *Oxford Journal of Archaeology*, vol. 2, no. 1 (1983), pp. 93–107.
32. *VCH* vol. 3, p. 24; *Gentleman's Magazine* (1816), Pt. 2, pp. 17–20.
33. A. Down, *Chichester Excavations 4*, pp. 51–3.
34. A. Down, *Chichester Excavations 5*, p. 134.
35. S.S. Frere, *Britannia* (1967), pp. 280–1.

Chapter Six

1. A. Down, *Chichester Excavations 5*, p. 128.
2. A. Down, *Chichester Excavations 2*, p. 113.
3. A. Down, *Chichester Excavations 5*, pp. 88–90.
4. M.G. Welch, 'Early Anglo-Saxon Sussex, vol. 1', *BAR* 112 (1), p. 256.
5. B.W. Cunliffe, 'Excavations at Portchester, vol. II, Saxon', *RRSAL* XXXIII, pp. 121–2.
6. A. Down and M.G. Welch, 'The pagan Saxon cemetery at Appledown, Compton, West Sussex', *Chichester Excavations 7* (forthcoming).

Bibliography

Aldsworth 1985	F.G. Aldsworth, 'Bignor Roman Villa (The Baths): Excavations in 1985', (Interim Report, WSCC & English Heritage).
Aldsworth and Rudling 1985	F.G. Aldsworth and D. Rudling, 'Bignor Roman Villa: Excavations in 1985 and Interim Report', WSCC.
Allen 1976	D.F. Allen, 'Did Adminius strike coins?' *Britannia* VII.
Applebaum 1975	S. Applebaum, 'Observations on the economy of the villa at Bignor', *Britannia* VI.
Barnes 1981	H. Barnes, 'The human skeletal remains from Eastgate Needlemakers', *Chichester Excavations 5.*
Bedwin and Holgate 1985	O. Bedwin and R. Holgate, 'Excavations at Copse Farm, Oving, West Sussex', *PPS* 51.
Bedwin & Pitts 1978	O. Bedwin and M.W. Pitts, 'The excavation of an Iron Age settlement at North Bersted, Bognor Regis, West Sussex, 1975–6', *SAC* 116.
Black 1983	E.W. Black, 'The Roman villa at Bignor', *Oxford Journal of Archaeology*, vol. 2, no.1.
– 1985	'The Roman buildings at Bosham', *SAC* 123.
– 1987	'The Roman Villas of South East England', *BAR* British Series 171.
Bogaers 1979	J.E. Bogaers, 'King Cogidubnus: Another reading of RIB 91', *Britannia* X.
Boon 1969	G. Boon, *Archaeologia* 102.
Bradley 1971	R. Bradley, 'A Field Survey of the Chichester Earthworks', in B.W. Cunliffe, 'Excavations at Fishbourne, vol. 1', *RRSAL*, XXVI.
Camden	W. Camden, *Britannia*, vol. 5.
Collins *et al.*	A.H. Collins, A.E. Wilson and C. Wilson, 'The Roman site at Sidlesham', *SAC* 111.
Corney 1984	M. Corney, 'A Field Survey of the Extra Mural region of Silchester', in M. Fulford, 'Silchester Defences 1974–80', *Britannia Monograph Series*, no. 5.
Cunliffe 1971	B.W. Cunliffe, 'Excavations at Fishbourne, vol. 1', *RRSAL.*
– 1973	*The Regni.*
– 1976	'Excavations at Portchester, vol. II: Saxon', *RRSAL* XXXIII.
– 1984	'Relations between Britain and Gaul in the 1st century B.C.' in 'Cross-Channel Trade between Gaul and Britain in the pre-Roman Iron Age', *Society of Antiquaries Occasional Paper* (New Series), IV.
Curwen 1954	E.C. Curwen, *The Archaeology of Sussex.*
Dallaway 1815	J. Dallaway, *History of the Western Division of the County of Sussex*, vol. 1.
Down and Rule 1971	A. Down and M. Rule, *Chichester Excavations 1.*
Down 1974	A. Down, *Chichester Excavations 2.*
– 1978	A. Down, *Chichester Excavations 3.*
– 1979	A. Down, *Chichester Excavations 4.*
– 1981	A. Down, *Chichester Excavations 5.*
– 1988	A. Down, *Chichester Excavations 6.*
Down and Welch (forthcoming)	A. Down and M. Welch, 'The pagan Saxon Cemetery at Appledown, Compton, West Sussex', *Chichester Excavations 7.*
Down (forthcoming)	A. Down, *Chichester Excavations 8.*
Frere 1967	S.S. Frere, *Britannia.*
– 1982	'Bignor Roman Villa', *Britannia* XIII.
– 1984	'British Urban Defences in Earthwork', *Britannia* XV.

Fulford   M. Fulford, 'Calleva Atrebatum: an Interim Report on the excavation of the
(forthcoming)   Oppidum, 1980–86', *PPS* 53.
Gentleman's Magazine, (1830), Part 2.
Green 1970   T.K. Green, 'Roman Tileworks at Itchingfield', *SAC* 108.
Harman (forthcoming)   M. Harman, 'The Anglo-Saxon burials from Appledown, Compton', in A.
                            Down and M.G. Welch, *Chichester Excavations 7*.
Hassall 1981   M.W.C. Hassall, 'The Purbeck marble inscription from Eastgate Needle-
                            makers', *Chichester Excavations 5*.
Hay 1804   A. Hay, *The History of Chichester*.
Henig and Nash 1982   M. Henig and D. Nash, 'Amminius and the Kingdom of Verica', *Oxford Journal
                            of Archaeology* vol. 1, no. 2.
Holmes 1962   J. Holmes, 'The Defences of Roman Chichester', *SAC* 100.
 – 1965   'Chichester, the Roman Town', *Chichester Papers*, no. 50.
King 1980   A. King, 'A Graffito from La Graufesenque', *Britannia* XI.
King and Soffe   A. King and G. Soffe, 'The Iron Age and Roman Temple at Hayling Island,
(forthcoming)   Hants., *Britannia Monograph Series*.
Levitan 1988   B. Levitan, 'The vertebrate remains from Chichester Cattlemarket', *Chichester
                            Excavations 6*.
McWhirr 1981   A. McWhirr, *Roman Gloucestershire*.
Margary 1973   I.D. Margary, *Roman Roads in Britain*.
Mitchell 1866   H. Mitchell, 'On the early traditions of Bosham', *SAC* 18.
Pitts 1979   M.W. Pitts, 'A Gazetteer of Roman sites', *SAC* 117.
Praetorius 1910   C.J. Praetorius, 'Paper on the Roman building near Pulborough, Sussex', *Proc.
                            Soc. Antiq.*, vol. 23.
Reynolds 1986   P.J. Reynolds, *Butser Ancient Farm Yearbook*.
Rudkin 1986   D.J. Rudkin, 'The excavation of a Romano-British site by Chichester Harbour,
                            Fishbourne', *SAC* 124.
Rudling 1984   D. Rudling, 'Excavations in Tarrant Street, Arundel, West Sussex', *Bulletin of
                            the Institute of Archaeology, University of London*.
 – 1986   D. Rudling *et al.*, 'The Excavation of a Roman Tilery on Great Cansiron
                            Farm, Hartfield, Sussex', *Britannia* XVII.
Scott 1938 & 1939   'Angmering Roman Villa', *SAC* 79 and 80.
Welch 1983   M.G. Welch, 'Early Anglo-Saxon Sussex, vol. 1', *BAR* 112, British Series.
Wells 1982   C. Wells, 'Romano-British Cemeteries at Cirencester: the Human burials',
                            Cirencester Excavations II.
White 1936   G.M. White, 'The Chichester Amphitheatre: Preliminary Excavations', *Ant.
                            J.* 16.
Wilson 1962   A.E. Wilson, 'Chichester Excavations 1958–60', *SAC* 100.
Winbolt 1932   S.E. Winbolt, 'The Roman Villa at Southwick', *SAC* 73.

Index